VIDEO
NATION

JEFFERSON GRAHAM

Peachpit
Press

Video Nation

A DIY guide to planning, shooting, and sharing great video from *USA TODAY*'s Talking Tech host Jefferson Graham

Peachpit Press
1249 Eighth Street
Berkeley, CA 94710
(510) 524-2178
Fax: (510) 524-2221

Find us on the Web at www.peachpit.com
To report errors, please send a note to errata@peachpit.com
Peachpit Press is a division of Pearson Education

Senior Editor: Karyn Johnson
Developmental Editor: Jacqueline Aaron
Copy Editor: Jacqueline Aaron and Kelly Kordes Anton
Production Editor: Becky Winter
Composition: Danielle Foster
Technical Editor: Nancy Blair
Proofreader: Kelly Kordes Anton
Indexer: Valerie Perry
Interior Design: Claudia Smelser
Cover Design: Charlene Will

ISBN-13: 978-0-321-83287-0
ISBN-10:   0-321-83287-6

9 8 7 6 5 4 3 2 1

Printed and bound in the United States of America

To my wife, Ruth, and my parents, Jerry and Judy.

ACKNOWLEDGMENTS

I need to send a number of shoutouts to people for their help with this book:

- To my loving wife Ruth, who watches all my videos and then tells me to brush my hair and stop talking so fast. She's also my number one fan. I'm hers too. And thanks to my artist/photographer son Sam Graham for taking the great back-cover photo.

- The terrific folks at USA TODAY, especially Jeremy Teres, for pushing me to go further with video than I'd done in the past and helping to get the "Talking Tech" spin-off, "Talking Your Tech," launched. A round of applause as well for Geri Coleman Tucker, Nancy Blair, Sam Meddis, Steve Elfers, and Ed Baig.

- Sean Fujiwara and David Medill, who have assisted me on most of the "Talking Tech" and "Talking Your Tech" video shoots discussed in this book. Thanks for the creativity, skill, and, most of all, for helping to carry all those bags.

- The team at Peachpit, my editors Karyn Johnson, Jacqueline Aaron, Kelly Anton, and the above-mentioned Nancy Blair, as well as marketing pros Damon Hampson and Laura Pexton Ross. I've never seen a smarter publishing company.

- Cris Bennett, Linda McLaughlin Figel, Margot Farris, Patty Gibson, Julia Levee, Nigesa Kamae, Richard and Lisa Goldstein, and Reza Hosseini all let me photograph them for the book—thanks for taking the time!

- Judson Coplan, Monica Sarkar, and the rest of the amazing Apple team—thanks for always being available to answer questions, even on the weekend.

- My mom, Judy Graham, for agreeing to have her son interview her for the book and use the video clips for Chapter 8; her life partner Mike Ansell for participating; and my dad, Jerry Graham, for buying me my first camera and guitar at age 13 and starting me down this path. Also thanks to my brother Jez for being my favorite subject to photograph growing up, and to Lily and Catherine as well.

- Speaking of guitars, some words of thanks to my favorite guitarists: Pat Metheny, Jim Hall, George Benson, and Robben Ford for keeping me company musically while writing the book.

- To my photo pals—Stephan Cooper, Brian Valente, and Syl Arena—for the fun shop talk over the last few months. Stephan—thanks for the great cover photo.

- Groucho, Harpo, Chico, Buster, Charlie, Harold, Lucy, Bugs, Daffy, Popeye, Donald, and Huey, Dewey, and Louie—thanks for all the laughs.

Jefferson Graham is a longtime technology columnist for *USA TODAY* and host, producer and editor of the *USA TODAY*'s "Talking Tech" and "Talking Your Tech" video shows, which feature interviews with tech newsmakers, reviews of the latest gadgets, and celebrity visits. Apple products such as the iPad, iPhone, and Final Cut Pro X were seen early on "Talking Tech," one of a small handful of outlets to get early peeks at the new Apple releases. Recent guests on "Talking Your Tech" have included Selena Gomez, Carson Daly, and Jeff Dunham; tech stars such as Zynga CEO Mark Pincus and Pandora's Tim Westergren; and, YouTube breakouts iJustine and the Annoying Orange himself, Dane Boedigheimer. All the shows are produced professionally on the same DIY budgets described in this book.

Jefferson is the author of nine books, including *Vegas: Live and In Person* and *Salesman of the Century* (with infomercial legend Ron Popeil). He is also an accomplished Manhattan Beach, California–based portrait photographer, videographer, and jazz guitarist.

CONTENTS

INTRODUCTION

All kinds of people today are creating video for the web. Whether you're a small business owner, a blogger, or a web show host, or if you're simply doing some marketing for your company or yourself, right now you may be all on your own in learning how to put that video together, make it look good, and get it to go viral.

Learning filmmaking and production techniques can be a daunting task because most books and resources cover productions with big budgets and multiple crew members. Resources that cover only the camera or video editing aren't particular helpful either if you don't know the basics about video production.

This is where *Video Nation* comes in. I wrote this book to provide the layman with real-world, practical advice, from what I learned over the years producing a minimum of two videos per week on a DIY budget for *USA TODAY*'s "Talking Tech" and "Talking Your Tech" shows.

In this book, you'll learn what equipment you need to get started to create your own "one-man band" productions, including advice on shooting with DSLRs, point-and-shoot cameras, and iPhones. You'll get the best techniques for setting up, preparing questions for, and interviewing a subject. I've included detailed descriptions of working with sound and lighting for a variety of indoor and outdoor scenarios. You'll even get to take your video to the next level by using multiple cameras.

Once you've shot your video, I give you step-by-step instructions for using editing programs such as Apple iMovie, Adobe Premiere Elements, and Final Cut Pro X. After that, you'll learn how to upload your video to YouTube, create a channel, market your video with Twitter and Facebook, and earn money from your efforts. Throughout the book, you'll get tips on developing fresh new ways to promote your business or yourself.

It's my hope that, after reading the book, you'll know how to create videos that look professional and also raise your profile in your business or your personal endeavors.

Videos Accompanying the Book

Throughout *Video Nation,* TV icons (such as the one shown in the margin here) indicate a video clip is available for you to watch. You can download the clips once you register your book at www.peachpit.com/videonation. More than 30 clips are available to show some of the concepts from the book in action, including how to set up a shoot, get better audio results, light an interview subject, and edit your video. You'll also see some behind-the-scenes videos of interviews with Mike Tyson, Adam Carolla, Valerie Bertinelli, Penn Jillette, J.B. Smoove, and more.

I'll add more videos to the resources page at www.peachpit.com/videonation, so make sure to check back for additional videos.

Each numbered video corresponds to an accompanying short video clip at www.peachpit.com/videonation.

EVERYBODY
IS A STAR

1

ON THE WEB, thanks to the explosion of online video, now anybody can be a star. You can host your own talk show, produce Internet news segments, or just talk into a webcam and throw the results on YouTube—complete with jerky shots of the camera being set up, turned on, and turned off. It's obvious most people don't care about making their videos look professional and polished on the web, but you do; otherwise you wouldn't be reading this book.

Perhaps you've been using your point-and-shoot camera to make videos, but you'd love to learn how to make them more polished. Or you own a small business, know you should be doing video marketing, but don't have $3000 to pay someone to produce weekly videos for you.

New and very affordable digital tools for shooting and editing video offer surprisingly good quality. As recently as five years ago, you needed thousands of dollars to invest in quality video gear to get started; these days that's not the case. Anyone with access to a video camcorder, a point-and-shoot camera, or an iPhone or iPad, can produce great-looking video.

In *Video Nation*, I describe the most common kinds of short-form web videos, talk about brainstorming for ideas, and show you how to make professional-looking segments using off-the-shelf digital tools that are probably sitting on your desk or in your pocket right now. If you want to graduate to the next level and work with more state-of-the-art gear, I'll show you how to do that, too.

BE YOUR OWN ONE-MAN BAND

Check out Jeff's introduction to *Video Nation* in the video at www.peachpit.com/videonation.

Since 2007 I have produced, edited, and hosted *USA TODAY*'s "Talking Tech" series (www.usatoday.com/tech/columnist/talkingtech) helming more than 300 episodes from start to finish (Figure 1.1). Originally my notion was for a weekly audio podcast series devoted to the world of consumer technology, but my bosses said they wanted it to be a web video series instead. Since I'm a ham and a gearhead, I was only too happy to oblige.

I've been shooting videos since the 1980s (editing that video footage on a VHS tape) and taking photos since the ripe old age of 13. Originally, "Talking Tech" was a bicoastal production, with me in Los Angeles and my colleague Ed Baig in New Jersey, and we would talk tech into our video cameras. Ed would send me his footage and I'd couple it with mine, usually edited with Adobe Premiere Elements, a consumer video-editing program.

Figure 1.1
USA TODAY's Jefferson Graham talks to newsmakers, celebrities, and consumers about how they use technology in their lives.

Then, over time, we started getting ambitious and added more production value, location shooting, and interviews to the show. Fast-forward to today. At this point, I churn out about three "Tech" videos a week, all from my garage in Manhattan Beach, California (*Figure* 1.2), using off-the-shelf consumer tools that include DSLRs (digital single-lens-reflex cameras), the iPhone, point-and-shoot cameras, and even the GoPro extreme wide-angle "helmet cam," favored by action-sports enthusiasts to capture their own high-intensity exploits with an amazing ultra-wide angle view.

Sometimes (but very rarely) we even shoot with a traditional video camcorder. Mix in tripod and monopod, microphones and audio recorder, lighting gear, a laptop, and video-editing software. That's all we need to produce little three-minute videos for the web, where the most popular ones—usually early reviews of new Apple products—have received more than 3 million views.

Film is considered a collaborative medium, with a director as the top visionary overseeing an army of actors (or interview-subjects for a documentary), camera shooters, lighting operators, sound engineers, and the like. But for web video, you're the guy or the gal, and you can do it all, if you want.

In the beginning, that's how I did it. But now, on the more polished pieces I have help; for my "Talking Tech" and "Talking Your Tech" pieces, I usually work with a camera operator. I write the segments, set up the shots, oversee the lighting and audio, and (usually) edit the final product. Yet I also still produce many segments by setting up the shot in the camera's viewfinder, pressing record, and then running back into place to record my piece. I've held up an iPhone or a Flip video camera (steady, of course) and talked directly into the phone or camera for my traditional "stand-up" shot—the one you've seen on TV a million times of a reporter in front of City Hall.

You, too, will probably start as a "one-man band," or you'll have a friend helping. You'll conceive of the total setup: you'll decide where to shoot and what kind of angles to use, you'll shoot the video, you'll appear on camera, and you'll edit the final product. I have no problem handling all of these chores, except for one—lining myself up in a camera viewfinder. I find that task really tough to pull off professionally. It's just really hard to compose a great shot when you're not behind the viewfinder.

For example, I did a stand-up at Apple headquarters after a press event—complete with the shot of me in front of the iconic Apple sign. But the logo bled out of the frame. I was too far to the left. I kept doing it over and over again, until I finally gave up and approached a photographer from a TV station—who was working on his own piece—and asked if he would be nice enough to give me a hand.

Another limitation of shooting solo is getting the same kind of natural human contact with the interviewee when the interviewer is stuck behind the camera viewfinder. It's often ideal to have the interviewer included in the shot as well (*Figure* 1.3). I have tips for how to get around that at the conclusion of this chapter, in the section "Real Life: Producing 'Talking Tech'."

Figure 1.3 This would be a tough shot to do alone. Get some help for those special shots.

Besides lining up the shot, zooming in at the right moment, and in general monitoring everything that's happening behind the camera, it's great to have a second person on hand to help carry the gear and set up lighting and audio. Not that you can't do it on your own; you certainly can. In any case, we'll explore all the ways you can make short videos by yourself or with a skeleton crew.

Through the years, I've suffered through every possible video and audio mistake and production mishap there is to endure—batteries running out of juice, losing the footage from a memory card, having lights blow on the spot—you name it. I hope you won't have to face such disasters, as I'll be pointing out in *Video Nation* what to do—and what not to do—to minimize mishaps and maximize success.

So if you've been watching the web versions of the Brian Williams, Diane Sawyer, and Scott Pelley newscasts, or the homegrown news reports on websites such as Patch.com and USAToday.com, and thought, "Hey, I can do that, too," I'll show you how to make it happen.

THE BASIC ELEMENTS OF A WEB VIDEO PRODUCTION

In the chapters to come, I'll cover the most common types of videos, various production styles, and what equipment you'll need to get started—from bare-bones optimal to wish-list, state-of-the-art great. Then I'll take you deeper into the process for creating great online video, with discussions on the following:

- Type of camera gear you might want to use
- Preproduction planning
- What to expect on production day
- Basic video editing
- Advanced video-editing techniques
- Exporting and sharing video
- Building an audience

Now, before we start getting into the nitty-gritty, let's take a brief look at the ten essential elements of workflow for making videos, which we'll go over in more explicit detail in upcoming chapters.

Figure 1.4

The author interviews Valerie Bertinelli for "Talking Your Tech."

Start with the Idea

If you're doing traditional journalism—an interview, for example, or a news story—you'll need to make contact with your subject and set up a time to meet (*Figure* 1.4). If you've got an original story in mind, map it out. How do you want to illustrate it? Who will be in it, and who (if anyone) will help you with camera operations? Remember that when watching web video, people's attention spans are even worse than when viewing TV. As much as we like to click a remote control to change the channel, our trigger finger on the mouse moves at an even greater speed. So keep the video short—two to three minutes, tops. Once you realize that you're not making *Gone with the Wind,* it'll be easier to visualize the handful of shots you'll need for your video. (I go into more detail on coming up with ideas and planning your production in Chapter 5.)

Go with Your Gear

You can use any digital tool to tell your story, whether it be an iPhone (*Figure* 1.5); a point-and-shoot camera; or a bigger, heavy-duty digital single-lens–reflex (DSLR) camera. A little lighting will go a long way toward making the images look crisper and sharper. And sound is a major issue. Forget about the dinky internal microphone on cameras—it will record every piece of sound in the neighborhood, instead of just focusing on the subject. You need to get audio from an external mic. Don't have a fortune to spend? Not a problem. I'll show you how to pull it off, with either an affordable mic or a separate audio recorder. (For more specifics on gear, see Chapters 3 and 4.) Next comes the all-important question: Where to shoot?

Figure 1.5 You can easily stabilize iPhones with a tripod.

Plan Your Shoot

First, *pick a location*. How do you decide where to shoot? The likeliest options are your home, your office, or an outdoor spot; each has its plusses and minuses. A home or office would give you the best options for lighting, as you could set up the shot there, but it could look bland. Shooting in public generally looks alive and gives you decent lighting, but you will get kicked out of most public places if you try to shoot a serious production on the premises without calling in advance for approval. No tripod, no lights, no big camera, and you just might get away with it. But try setting up anything in a Target, supermarket, shopping mall, or chain restaurant, and you will get booted out, quick. (Look for more on preproduction planning in Chapter 5.) A locally owned restaurant might let you shoot, if it's not too busy (think early in the morning). Audio-wise, anything outside is rife with problems—you'll be competing with people talking, horns buzzing, and birds squawking. But the lighting is usually perfect. If you can find a quiet corner of the world outside, go for it. Otherwise, the options you're left with are homes and offices.

Second, plan to *be early*. There's nothing worse than having a video shoot setup for 10:30 a.m. and arriving to start filming at 10:30 a.m. Part of the deal is that you have to arrive to the location at least one hour ahead of time to set up. This is a basic rule you'll have to adhere to. Setting up the camera and checking sound and lighting takes time, and it's best to be prepared when your subject is looking in your face and ready to go. This is vital.

Shoot with Savvy

The sad reality about photography is that even though cameras are small enough to be handheld, most videos can't get away with the handheld look. It's just too jerky and distracting, even with tools like built-in stabilization. Some people think it's cool to show jerky video on their websites; I don't. I recommend that, for any production you use a tripod to steady the image—even for point-and-shoot cameras or the iPhone. For the mobile minded, look at a monopod, which is a tripod with one leg that offers nimble steadiness (*Figure 1.6*). I get into the nitty-gritty of shooting in Chapter 4.

Figure 1.6 This monopod is steady and light enough to carry along with your other equipment.

Interview Intelligently

If you're producing an interview, think ahead about what you want to ask, and how to get the response you need. For instance, if you're talking to a restaurant owner about his most popular dish, you want to hear him repeat the question in his answer—for example, "My most popular dish is fish and chips," instead of just answering, "Fish and chips." This will make it a smooth insert in editing, without having to also hear the setup question.

Plan ahead by writing a list of possible questions to ask, while remaining flexible enough to make up new ones on the spot based on your conversation. We'll dive into this in more depth in Chapter 2.

Master Watchability: B-roll

The web, like TV, is a visual medium. People don't mind seeing someone talking for a little bit, but to make sure it doesn't get boring, you need to insert secondary shots to keep the action moving. This is called "B-roll," and it dates back to the early days of film, when the master shot was the A-roll, and other shots (medium, wide, and so on) were on another reel, the B-roll. It's B-roll that makes the story visual. Take a good look at any TV news show such as "60 Minutes," and you see very little of the actual interview in the piece—but you do hear it. You may see the subject speak a sentence or two, but most of the talking takes place behind the visuals that tell the story. For instance, I shot an interview in 2011 with a Coca-Cola executive talking about the company's use of Facebook to reach customers. What did I do to make the piece come to life with visuals? During the shoot, we looked for anything of interest—Coke cans and bottles, a Coke vending machine, Coke signs on the wall, the subject taking a drink of Coke, the interviewer and subject in a wide shot, the subject showing Coke's Facebook page and so on. During editing, we add more: images of Coke's Facebook page (*Figure 1.7*), Coke's website, and some video of Coke TV ads (readily available on sites such as YouTube). (For details on what gear works for B-roll, see Chapter 4.)

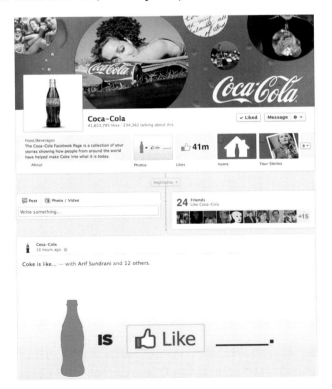

Figure 1.7 It's easy to grab screenshots like this one for additional B-roll.

Figure 1.8 iMovie is a cheap and easy video editing solution.

Perfect Postproduction

Video footage takes up massive amounts of storage space (think gigabytes, not megabytes), and these days it tends to be memory-card based, a huge innovation after the days of using tapes.

Today, you can transfer footage from memory cards to your computer or external hard drive in minutes. However, once you clear the card, you'll need a second copy of the footage, just in case something goes wrong with your drive. (And it will—that's guaranteed. I had four storage hard drives die on me recently.) So be sure to back up the footage before you begin editing. (For more details on postproduction, see Chapters 7 and 8.)

Edit with Ease

For most of my "Tech" videos, I spend about eight hours from start to finish in editing. The easy part for me is depicting the story and tracing it from beginning to end. What generally takes the most time is adding the graphics, titles, B-roll, and the like. The simplest and cheapest video-editing programs, such as Apple iMovie and Windows Movie Maker, could be frustrating for our productions in "Talking Tech" (*Figure 1.8*). They (without tweaks) have only one track of video, and thus no B-roll or audio on a second track, unless you employ workarounds. (I have a simple fix for iMovie, which I will explain in depth in Chapter 8, that will allow you to add insert shots and make the program usable for our needs. I have no workaround for Windows Movie Maker.)

If you're willing to shell out $50 to $100 for Adobe Premiere Elements (for Mac or Windows) or Sony Vegas (for Windows), both have decent entry-level video-editing programs that let you do multitrack video editing. Expect to spend most of your time in this phase, hunched over the computer, as this is where you really make the video come to life.

Figure 1.9 The sharing feature in Adobe Premiere Elements.

Share It with the World

Once you're finally finished, you're ready to share your video. As I discuss in Chapter 9, many video programs have a Share tab with instant exports to YouTube, Vimeo, Facebook, and other popular online destinations (*Figure* 1.9). I prefer saving the file to a specific place on my hard drive so I'll know where to find it later. Perhaps you'll need to upload it into an FTP program, with free online file transfer software such as Filezilla, or upload it to an online transfer site such as Dropbox, for sending to a friend or client. (You'll learn more about uploading your video to sharing sites such as YouTube in Chapter 10.)

Track Your Success

The great thing about the Internet is that you know instantly whether you have a hit or not. YouTube, Vimeo, and other video sites show you instantly how many views you have (for more on this, see Chapter 10). Some videos take off virally, to millions of views, but most don't. For yours to get a huge number of views, you'll have to promote it by posting links to the video in every conceivable place you can think of—Twitter, Facebook, bulletin boards, and the like.

REAL-LIFE SCENARIO: PRODUCING "TALKING TECH"

Now let me take you through a typical "Tech" interview, to show you how we put everything into motion, step by step. In summer 2011, I traveled from Los Angeles to Palo Alto (about eight hours away by car) to do a piece on Facebook, and how businesses could use the social network to increase their sales and have better communication with their customers (*Figure* 1.10).

Figure 1.10 This interview with Facebook can be found at the *USA TODAY* website at www.usatoday.com.

Red-hot social network Facebook is a great place to visit—as so many people are interested in seeing what the Facebook headquarters look like. Video adds so much more depth than just a standard print story. The trick is getting typically closed-up Facebook to open up and allow us free reign in showing off its HQ to the world.

I combined the Facebook shoot with a visit to Apple, in nearby Cupertino, to see a top-secret mock retail store, where Apple wanted me to see some cool new enhancements. However, Apple refused to let me shoot!

For these pieces, I drove up to the Bay Area with my camera bag, sound bag, tripod, and monopod. (Driving is my preferred mode of travel when lugging lots of gear.) I didn't have any serious, experienced help to produce the piece—it was sort of "one-man-band plus." But that's why I'm telling you about it. You could easily use this setup with a friend in nine out of ten situations.

A new hire, Jeremy, had just joined *USA TODAY* and was in San Francisco visiting. I asked (begged, actually) him to come along and give me a hand.

"But I don't know anything about photography or how to shoot professional video," he protested.

"Don't worry, I'll set everything up for you. You know how to use a point-and-shoot camera, right?"

Jeremy nodded.

"You'll be fine."

All I needed from Jeremy was some B-roll. As long as the footage was steady, I would have something to cut to, to make the video look professional (or at least semiprofessional), as opposed to having just a straight talking head, which, let's face it, gets old fast.

We drove up together to the Facebook HQ and entered the building, me lugging my camera bag, tripod, monopod, and small Canon point-and-shoot camera—the S95, which just happens to shoot in full 1080p HD with amazing quality (but you'll learn more about gear in Chapters 3 and 4). Facebook wanted us to do the interview in one of those awful, pure white conference rooms that both corporate America and even hip, trendy companies such as Facebook and Google seem to adore.

Pure white everywhere. Like going to heaven.

But boooorrring.

I liked the front lobby, where a Facebook grafitti wall invites guests to sign their name. "It has to be in the conference room," informed the publicist, Cindy, who was our initial Facebook contact. I took another look at the white room, and figured that if I zoomed in on Emily White, our Facebook executive, it might not be too bad. I'd just have to get lots of B-roll to liven it up.

The room had enough ambient light that I was able to use the available light for the interview—which is good, as I had inadvertently left my lights back home in Los Angeles! If the room had been truly dark and dreary, I would have taken Emily outside—had the publicist approved—perhaps in front of Facebook.

I opened up my tripod and set it up directly behind me, over my head, so that the camera was pointing directly at Emily White. This way I could speak to her and still make eye contact. This is crucial. I hate seeing video interviews with people when the camera looks at the side of their face. I want to see both eyes.

For sound, I put a wireless lavalier microphone on Emily's blouse, and the wireless mic receiver (they work in tandem) connected directly to my camera. During my chat with Emily, I asked Jeremy to roam with the point-and-shoot atop a monopod, which isn't as steady as a tripod, but much better than handheld. With the monopod he could get secondary shots. Even if he didn't know a lick about photography, he could still get a wide shot of us from the left and right, shoot from above and below, and just have some fun. (Besides, I needed the tripod for the master Emily White shot.)

After the interview, Facebook agreed to let us spend a few minutes gathering the crucial B-roll. I had Jeremy get a shot of Emily showing me a Facebook page on her computer. I positioned the point-and-shoot, and had Jeremy get Emily and me walking in front of the graffiti wall, signing our names and talking. This sounds like bland stuff, but watch the news—most videos always show the subject and interviewer walking and talking. Anything to get movement.

Once we did the walk and talk, Emily had to leave for a meeting. So I picked up the point-and-shoot and finished up with shots of the Facebook logo up front, people entering and exiting the lobby, and a close-up of a "Like us on Facebook" sticker on the wall.

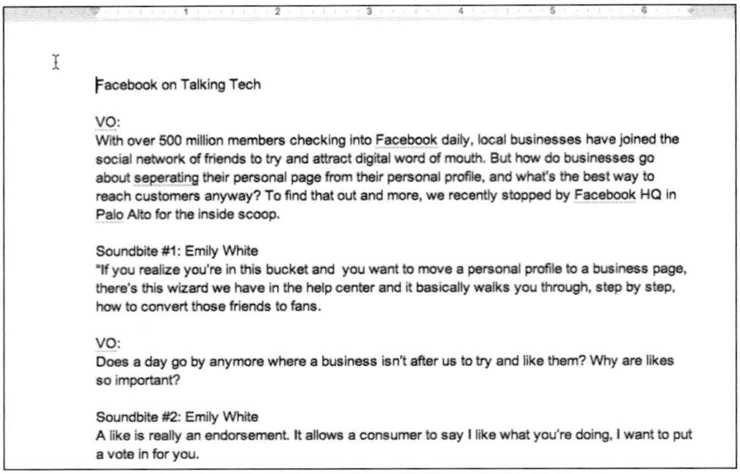

Figure 1.11 Putting together a script is easy in any word processing program.

The figure shows a word processing document with the following text:

> Facebook on Talking Tech
>
> VO:
> With over 500 million members checking into Facebook daily, local businesses have joined the social network of friends to try and attract digital word of mouth. But how do businesses go about seperating their personal page from their personal profile, and what's the best way to reach customers anyway? To find that out and more, we recently stopped by Facebook HQ in Palo Alto for the inside scoop.
>
> Soundbite #1: Emily White
> "If you realize you're in this bucket and you want to move a personal profile to a business page, there's this wizard we have in the help center and it basically walks you through, step by step, how to convert those friends to fans.
>
> VO:
> Does a day go by anymore where a business isn't after us to try and like them? Why are likes so important?
>
> Soundbite #2: Emily White
> A like is really an endorsement. It allows a consumer to say I like what you're doing, I want to put a vote in for you.

Once home, I imported the footage and started assembling more B-roll. What is standard for any video about a website is a bunch of screen shots of the website. I went to Facebook and grabbed some images of Facebook pages (press Shift-Command+3 on the Mac or press the Print Screen key on a Windows keyboard, and cut and paste the copy into Paint or Photoshop to save it).

I played back the entire interview with Emily White and transcribed it so I could pull out the sound bites for the script, then banged out a script (*Figure* 1.11). I approach video scriptwriting the same way I do for newspaper articles: I tell viewers up front why they'll want to watch—in this case, for a story about how small businesses can use Facebook—and I use sound bites where you would see quotes in an article.

Then I use B-roll to illustrate Emily's thoughts.

The hook, again, is that Facebook is offering tips on how to use the social network to promote a small business. We illustrate this with any images of Emily, myself, and Facebook we can find. My rule for videos is that if the subject or narrator mentions something of any significance at all, we should show it on the screen. So if Emily White tells why the Like button is so important, we show an image of the Like button. If the narrator talks about visiting Facebook headquarters for the interview, we show the Facebook lobby and people walking in and out (movement again!).

Once the B-roll was in place (*Figure* 1.12), I added the final touches: the graphics of the show's open and close, the theme song, and the *USA TODAY* watermark (that little logo you see on the bottom of computer and TV screens—networks

Figure 1.12 A clip of the B-roll as shown in Final Cut Pro.

use them all the time on their shows, too). I add the *snipe,* the little graphic that goes under Emily White's name so you can see the text better. I *exported* (video-ese for "save" and "share") the final version as a lower-res H.264 QuickTime file (*USA TODAY* uses the Apple platform) with "good" quality and sound in mono at AAC. (I cover more details on sharing your final product in Chapter 10.)

A full version could be as big as 2 gigabytes, compared with about 100 mega-bytes for the H.264 version. For video, you don't need to display it in the highest resolution because that would just slow down the loading time and drive your viewers crazy. Most media outlets use the H.264 format because it is a lower reso-lution that loads fast and looks great.

After the export, I watched the video all the way through to make sure there were no mistakes.

But there are always mistakes. I've never exported a video just once. Perhaps the watermark didn't come through in the right position, or maybe I spelled one of the names wrong. Was the audio on the narration track too low? Yes, as always. Have to fix it. Did I make the music too high? Every time. Did one of my transitions look odd? Hopefully not, but there's at least one that needs to be tweaked. Fix it, do another export, and watch again.

Once satisfied, I shipped it off to *USA TODAY* and it soon went online.

So that's my workflow for this particular show and it's similar to how my other segments work, too. Ready to get started on yours, and bring your video to the web? Let's turn the page and get started.

WHAT TYPE OF VIDEO ARE YOU PRODUCING?

2

THE FIRST QUESTION you need to answer as you begin your foray into video production is what type of project do you hope to make? There are so many possibilities. Full-length feature? Oral history of your parents? Those examples are great for long-form projects. But for shorter, online video—the focus of this book—there are several tried-and-true favorites: the parody or comedy, the advertorial, the product demo, the vlog (video blog), the webisode, and the interview.

STYLES OF WEB VIDEO

You can produce any of these styles of video—by yourself or with a helper—using the one-camera shoot (explained in detail in Chapter 6). Whatever type you choose, I'll provide you with the know-how to create a professional-looking video.

The Parody or Comedy

Usually related to a hot music video or movie, or something political, parody videos are huge online. Think about any silly video on the Funny or Die, My Damn Channel, or CollegeHumor websites, where pros offer polish, usually with some mix of celebrity. Or, consider popular videos on YouTube, where some amazing music takeoffs by the likes of iJustine, Annoying Orange (*Figure 2.1*), and Shane Dawson get millions of views by offering their takes on hits by the hottest acts of the moment—such as Lady Gaga, Ke$ha, or the Black Eyed Peas. As viewers, we don't have to wait for the latest funny video from Weird Al Yankovic anymore. No, now we're all Weird Al Yankovic.

The Advertorial

The web is full of advertorials for businesses. For example, you might see a video of a restaurant owner or a car dealer showing off the goods, urging folks to come in (*Figure 2.2*). YouTube and other websites are full of "straight" commercials, in which the owner talks into the camera and urges folks to stop by—as well as comedy commercials, which, unlike on TV, can be as edgy and as long as you please on the web.

Figure 2.1 Annoying Orange reached over a billion views for his YouTube videos.

The Product Demo

Software manufacturers, camera makers, and the like do product demos all the time (*Figure 2.3*). Having trouble with your new app or camera? Just search for the problem in Google, and up pops a video demo, with an announcer off-camera, narrating over video shots of the computer screen as they show you the work-around to your problem. Product demos are also commonly used to launch new products, to help users get a visual understanding of how they work. Google does this every time it makes a new update to its website. New gadgets launch with YouTube channels devoted to showing every side of the product, including how to plug it in and enjoy it.

Figure 2.3 Product demos, such as this one by Scott Kelby, are another genre of video that you can create with desktop tools.

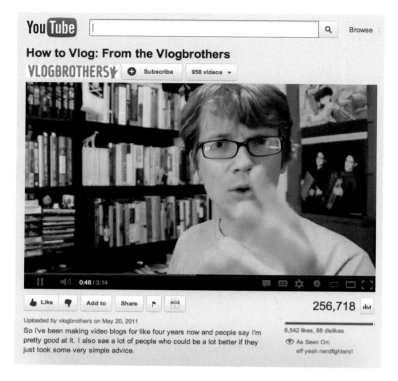

Figure 2.4 There are vlogs on just about anything, from book reviews to political events to coverage on a teenager's social life.

The Vlog

A video blog, or vlog, features a host staring into the camera, usually from his or her home, talking about the events of the day and whatever else is on his or her mind (*Figure 2.4*). Vlogs are quite popular on YouTube, usually as "second" channels—a place where YouTube stars such as iJustine or Shane Dawson chat about the events of their day. They require no production. Just set up your shot and talk away. But don't forget to edit out the moments when you turn the camera on and off!

The Webisode

Webisodes constitute an ongoing, weekly series, usually a comedy or behind-the-scenes show with musicians such as Taylor Swift or Lady Antebellum, that involves a cast and writing crew (*Figure 2.5*). Since this book focuses on productions that you can produce yourself without a cast and crew, we won't focus on webisodes.

Figure 2.5 Webisodes are often weekly series that involve a crew of writers and a cast.

Figure 2.6 Terry White shows how to use the iPad in this tutorial.

The Tutorial

Another common type of online video is the tutorial (*Figure 2.6*). You would make this type of video if, for example, you had a cooking show and wanted to show off your amazing recipes. Or maybe you have a talent for beauty tips (makeup videos attract millions of views). Or perhaps you're like my mother, who enjoys producing how-to-knit videos.

Many folks create their tutorials as a straight, unrehearsed conversation, focusing the camera on their hands as they do it; many of the best tutorials focus on hands demonstrating something. Alternatively, you could write a script, type it into the I-Prompt-Pro teleprompter app, and read along as you demonstrate. Heck, you could even save yourself $2 and type your script into the computer, in a big font. Just focus the camera on yourself so that the computer screen is out of the way, and read aloud after pressing record.

The Interview

News-style interviews on YouTube and other websites are just like what we've seen on TV for decades. The traditional interview is often presented in an amateurish way on websites, with the interviewer off-camera throwing questions to the subject, while holding the camera jerkily in his or her hand. You're aiming for something better. We'll take a look at the basic setup of an interview in the next section.

PRODUCING AN INTERVIEW

Check out the video at www.peachpit. com/videonation for more on this shot with Mike Tyson.

The interview is the oldest type of video known to man. Just ask the 2,000 Year Old Man himself, Mel Brooks, who spun his comedic tales on audio records in the 1960s by answering questions posed by interviewer Carl Reiner. TV's first programs—such as NBC's "Today" and "The Tonight Show"—featured newsmakers and celebrities responding to questions posed by the hosts. For the web, you can easily produce an online interview with as little as a point-and-shoot or iPhone camera (see Chapter 4). You'll get a more professional-looking result using a multicamera setup, with one camera on the subject, another on the interviewer, and ideally a wide shot of the two as seen in *Figure 2.7* (also see Chapter 7).

But let's start with the basics of interviewing. (We'll get into more details on shooting an interview in Chapters 6 and 7.)

Figure 2.7
This wide shot includes both the author and Mike Tyson, making for a more interesting shot to use during editing.

Booking the Interview

Where do you find your "talent"? Seeking someone to interview in your video is as simple as calling your subject and asking for the time. Why wouldn't the gardening expert want to appear on camera and show off his expertise? For one, it's a big ego builder. And two, it's free publicity, which could translate into more sales for the shop.

TIP Before you call the local pizza king or top town cobbler to set up an interview and run over with your camera and gear in tow, do a dry-run interview with a friend or family member. Give it a whirl it in the living room. Do a version sitting down and standing up. Get comfortable asking questions. Have a list of questions ready to refer to. Even if you don't look down at them during the interview, the act of writing them out will help you prepare.

Interview Tips: The Five Best Questions

Start with the obvious: who, what, where, when, and why. Those are the five basic questions in journalism, and they always work.

Say you will be interviewing a local handyman about the various services he offers. Here are some questions you could ask:

- What's his name? (Who.)
- What does he do? (What.)
- Which areas does he serve? (Where.)
- How busy is he during these recessionary times? (When.)
- How has he become one of the most sought-after handymen in town? (Why.)

Now flip the question to a nearby Taco Truck and it won't be much different:

- What's the name of the establishment? (Who.)
- What fare do you serve? (What.)
- Where do you generally park this truck? (Where.)
- What's the best time to get to the truck before the huge lines appear? (When.)
- Why are these tacos so popular? What's your special way of making them? (Why.)

Of course you can expand beyond the five questions with anything you'd like to know. For instance, if it's the profile of the Taco Truck, I'd want to know a little background on the Taco Trucker: What he was doing before he started the truck, and what a normal day at the truck is like. What time do they start prepping the food? How many tacos will they churn out of the truck from morning to night? If the truck is always around, when does he get the supplies?

Beyond the questions, remember that what your viewers really want to see is the inside of the truck itself. I'd bring in the camera for lots of shots of tacos being created and delivered to customers, busy worker bees inside the truck doing their jobs, and mouth-watering close-ups of tortillas, lettuce, cheese, meat, and all other sorts of taco-oriented goodness.

In asking the questions, especially for a one-camera interview, the trick is that you want each sound bite to be freestanding, so it can be added to the final version in editing without needing to hear your question to set up the answer.

If you ask, "What time do you get here in the morning to set up?" and he says, "Six," ask him to repeat your question in the answer. "I get here every morning at six to open up."

Taking It to the Web

I'm assuming many readers of *Video Nation* are bloggers or Facebookers who would love to post some great-looking videos. Aren't there tons of favorite local stores, places (an amazing park), or events in your community worth showing off to the world?

Think your blog can't compete with the local newspaper? Why should the garden shop give you the time of day? Yes, you may only have 1,000 monthly visitors, compared with a daily newspaper circulation of 50,000 or more. But in this era of social media, while your initial post may have just a few hundred readers, the business owner can take that link and throw it on his blog as well. And Facebook (*Figure 2.8*). And Twitter.

You get the idea.

Figure 2.8 This restaurant site has linked to other bloggers, reviews on Facebook, thus giving them a bigger "circulation."

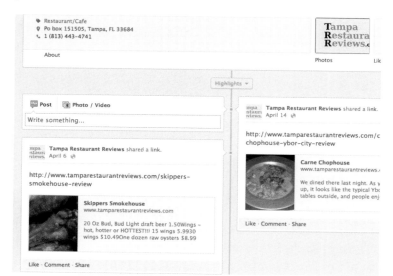

Your friends can link to it, and the next thing the business owner knows, Google has found the links, and every time there's a search for the garden center, your blog post just might be in the top five listings. Your blog has more weight than you realize. Use it to full advantage, with great-looking video reports. Google often places video links with thumbnails in its search results next to traditional text links—so your video piece could really stand out.

This brings us to the most common web video production format, the one-camera shoot, which you can use to produce not just interviews but all the video productions mentioned in this chapter.

PRODUCING A SMALL-BUSINESS VIDEO

So you've got a business and want to get in on the video action.You're in good company. According to the market tracker Ad-ology Research, 45 percent of small businesses plan to get way more involved with online video in 2012—and even more so in future years. And why not? A website really shines when it features a video greeting from the owner, testimonials from customers, demonstrations of what's for sale, and the like. And beyond the website, your customers are hanging out at Facebook, Twitter, and YouTube, where it's as simple to post a video as it is to put up a photo.

In this section, we'll look at the importance of taking your ideas directly to the web, either by yourself or with a helper. We'll look at how viral ads work and how to shape your idea into a shoot.

Promoting Your Business

Let's flip the interview around and look at producing a video aimed at promoting a small business, produced by the entrepreneur, and featuring the owner of the shop. Luckily, if you're in that position, you already have help—your employees.

Let's say you are Anthony Boswell, the garden expert, and you want to showcase your nursery with a video tour of sorts. It's a much cheaper way to advertise—after all, YouTube is free, while newspapers, magazines, radio, and TV ads cost in the thousands. All you need to start producing is video gear (or a student who has equipment and is willing to work cheap). I'd like to believe you're willing to invest in some quality equipment (camera, lighting, and audio; see Chapter 3), because over the long run you'll be creating so many pieces that it will be worth your while.

NOTE The key to promotional videos is to make them entertaining and educational. As a viewer, I'll watch if I learn something.

Taking Your Ideas Directly to the Web

You know who your audience is—your customers. And you want to reach them where they are. Your website is a great first place to start, and best of all, you can take the video you produce for your site, and place it easily on YouTube, Facebook, and Twitter as well. (Once you upload it to YouTube, the Google-owned video powerhouse directs you to easily "share" the video in other places, either via a link—which I find works best—or by just clicking the Share button and letting YouTube know where you want it to go. For more details about sharing your video, see Chapter 10.)

Speaking to Your Customers

In these videos, you have the opportunity to talk directly to both your existing fan (customer) base, and thousands of potential would-be customers, with straight chatter. Without the filter of a TV station, newspaper, or magazine, you can tell them directly who you are, what you're about, and why you do what you do.

You can talk about why you got in business and why you sell your particular product; show them your home office, factory, or storefront; introduce them to coworkers; and demonstrate the product. Once you get a rhythm going, you can start branching out into other areas, like reviews of products that relate to your industry, a great movie you just saw, or why you love living in your hometown.

The possibilities are endless.

Effective approaches

What I would like to see as a viewer of a garden shop video is something that shows me why Boswell is the green thumb expert. The target audience is composed of people who are into gardening, so naturally they'd all like to learn something from Boswell.

The videos should include content like this:

- Background details. How did you get started and become passionate about gardening?

- Think long-term. There should be at least 50 episodes devoted to different subjects such as varieties of plants and vegetables, when to plant and when not to, how to make sure they grow, and how to deal with obstacles such as hungry animals.
- Show us around the shop. Have some fun, and make it entertaining. Bring us to places we may not notice when we come in.

Content to avoid

Here's what we shouldn't see from you, Boswell, as a garden shop proprietor:

- Sales. My email box fills up every morning with ads from Amazon (the worst offender), Barnes & Noble, My Publisher, Shutterfly, and many other e-tailers, with subject lines telling me of once-in-a-lifetime offers. I get so many, I won't open any of them. Ever.
- A traditional ad that says "We're the best place in town, because we have a bigger/better/smarter [*take your pick*] selection."

Sell subtly

Even though I said not to make it an ad, you could do one in the following way: Do an episode in a particular section of the shop and tell us why you're there. Maybe your best-sellers are vegetables, and you're in the low-volume herbs section. Tell us that they don't move like the other items, but that you'd like to turn that around. Explain why herbs are undersung and should be more visible.

Production-wise, I could see you standing at the nursery and talking to the camera, as long as you include plenty of B-roll to keep the focus on the real star (no offense)—the product.

Take it to the next level by going on the road

Who's to say that you have to do all your video pieces at the nursery? Why not produce some episodes in a favorite customer's backyard? Do you have any amazing success stories to show? Why not interview your customers about them?

Ed Kaminsky is a real estate agent in my home town, Manhattan Beach, California, where he produces weekly videos aimed at garnering new home buyers and sellers.

What I like about his videos—which are anything but slick—is that while, naturally, he sells himself and his services, he also thinks outside the box to go beyond basic real estate, with informative community-based videos that appeal to a wider audience. He offers all this while subtly selling himself as the expert. He puts a tripod on the ground, lines up his Flip video camera or Nikon DSLR, presses record, and talks directly to the viewer.

"The more information I provide them, the better they understand that I am likely their best choice for real estate consulation when they need it," he says.

Kaminsky has parked in front of a local supermarket to shoot a piece on a new plastic-bag ban in Manhattan Beach, and what that means for consumers. He shot from one of Manhattan Beach's car-less "walk streets," to show what life is like there.

His bottom line: More videos equal higher visibility in Google and other search engines. His search engine optimization (or SEO—that is, tweaking a site to make sure it rises above the clutter) has "dramatically improved," from posting blog items and videos. "We are moving up the ranks," he says.

Kaminsky's videos, at youtube.com/edkaminskytv, show what can be done with no budget and a little brain power.

Ideas for Any Business

Perhaps as a small-business owner, you think, "Well, sure, gardening is a natural topic for multiple episodes, but *my* business doesn't have as much to talk about." *Au contraire*. Even in the age of online shopping, there are still huge crowds in stores—we haven't fled them all. And there's lots there to keep us interested (*Figure 2.9*).

Banking

Sure, the big bankers are sometimes perceived as evil. But if you're a small-town banker, why not play up the Main Street atmosphere? Introduce us to the owner, as well as the staff. I'd do a weekly series just on the tellers and their stories, hosted by the bank owner or manager. That would go a long way to showcase the difference between you and a national chain—a faceless Chase, Wells Fargo, or Bank of America.

Food

Meet the chef and servers at any restaurant. Share some recipes with us. Show us what went into the creation of a new dish—for example, why are sweet-potato fries in now? Interview customers about their favorite choices. Visit the local independent special grocery store—whether that be the farmers market, a neighborhood organic shop, or a great old mom-and-pop grocer—if they still exist. Ask them about the under-the-radar fruits and vegetables. Get to know the person behind the counter making the takeout sandwiches. What's the most popular sandwich, day in and day out, and how many of them do they make an hour? Talk to the owner of the shop about what it's like to be an independent in a world run by the Safeways and Vons.

See Jeff and a dry cleaner owner brainstorm on ideas for a video, and learn some things not to do along the way in the video at www.peachpit.com/videonation.

Figure 2.9 An industrious dry cleaner creates a unique video for his business.

See more about Fundy in the video at www.peachpit.com/videonation.

Andrew "Fundy" Funderburg sells software targeted to photographers, and he has tons of competition in a crowded field. So he turns to video promotion to stand out from the pack, churning out at least three self-produced videos a week from his Fundy Software offices in Portland, Oregon.

Many videos are demos of his products, with detailed tips on how to use them, but like Kaminsky, he branches out—with photography book reviews, interviews with photographers, reviews of photography labs, and tips on running a successful email marketing campaign.

"People are lazy," he says, when asked why he puts so much time into producing his videos. "They don't want to read. But they don't mind sitting and watching a little video instead of reading something."

He must be doing something right. As of early 2012, his videos have a combined 160,000 views—not bad for free marketing.

Each week Funderburg produces a minimum of three videos aimed at subtly selling his software for photographers. He produces everything from product demos to reviews of new books by photographers. When I interviewed him recently, he shared what "content marketing" means to him, told me what gear he uses, and discussed how he produces and shares his videos.

JG: How do you do content marketing?

AF: It's using good content to enhance your brand, to hopefully get them to buy your product. If everything on your blog is about your product, nobody will come. Our end users are portrait and wedding photographers. Anything we can do to help them out benefits us. So we do product and book reviews, tips on marketing, anything of value.

JG: What's your gear setup?

AF: I use a $500 Olympus Pen Mini camera with its $90 microphone attachment and a $20 Home Depot construction light. (Update: After this interview was conducted, Fundy went out and bought a more elaborate Westcott lighting system.)

JG: You're in the photography business. Why so low tech?

AF: To save money. There's no reason to spend big money on gear for this. Most modern cameras, even the cheapest ones, can shoot great HD video. The thing you really need is a real microphone to make it sound good.

JG: *What about post-production?*

AF: I edit on the iMac with Final Cut Pro X, and for screen-capture videos I use ScreenFlow software.

JG: *Do you produce your videos in true one-man-band fashion? Do you line yourself up, press record, and then jump in front of the camera?*

AF: I have the camera on a tripod, and have someone in my office start and stop the camera. When we're done, I load the video into the computer, drop in our intro and outro into Final Cut Pro X, and upload the video directly to YouTube from Final Cut.

JG: *I love that you take your small-business videos to another level by actually doing interviews with photographers via Skype. It's low tech, but it works.*

AF: They're fun. I use ScreenFlow to capture the screen, which shows both me and the photographer.

JG: *Has making videos helped your business?*

AF: A ton. Without it, we would really be hurting. They engage people so much.

JG: *How do you come up with video ideas?*

AF: Ideas come to me when I'm sitting around, driving, excercising, jogging. The ideas flow pretty easily.

JG: *What advice do you have for other small businesses looking to get into video?*

AF: Get a cheap camera that you can attach an external microphone to, and start doing it. It's one of those things that you just jump in, start doing it, and you get better at it.

Furniture shop

We see the ads on TV—lots of sales, great prices, rows and rows of furniture. But let's go beyond that and learn something. What's the most popular entry-level couch for newlyweds these days? Tell us about it, show it to us, make us want to sit in it and give it a try. You could do this straight, with the owner talking to the camera. Or you could show us customers taking a seat on the couch and expressing great comfort. You could jump into the frame and have a casual conversation with the customer—or us.

Give your audience useful, beyond-the-norm information, such as where couches are made these days, and how long it takes for them to arrive to our homes. You could direct the series to newlyweds or new divorcées, with episodes on couches, dinette sets, and bedroom gear.

In terms of production, employees will help you behind the camera, so you're good there. The key is to keep it moving. I'd want to see lots of shots of the owner/manager walking around the furniture shop, from couch to chair, from armoire to ottoman.

PRODUCING A PARODY

Nothing goes viral more quickly than a video making fun of a newsmaker, celebrity, hot music video, or band. In this section I'll disect some of the most popular YouTube parodies and explain how you, too, can make them. Remember that to get your idea out there, you don't need fancy equipment and a cast. You can do it all yourself. All you need is a green screen to superimpose yourself over a background, the ability to edit it in video-editing software (which I'll talk about in Chapters 8 and 9), and an area to film additional material, whether it be in a home or on location.

How the Pros Do It

YouTube stars such as iJustine, Shane Dawson, and VenetianPrincess have made careers out of spoofing celebrities, from Shakira and Beyoncé to the Black Eyed Peas, Rihanna, and Justin Bieber (*Figure 2.10*). All you need is a hot song and a karaoke instrumental track to sing over.

With a green screen backdrop, in video editing you can superimpose any background of your choice. Most of the pop music parodies feature YouTubers prancing in front of a green screen, with new locations superimposed behind them in the editing.

Figure 2.10 YouTube sensations iJustine and Shane Dawson have made careers out of their popular parodies.

Topical videos take an easy-to-lampoon subject—actor Alec Baldwin getting booted off an airplane for refusing to turn off his iPhone, presidential candidates doing silly things (womanizing, flip-flopping, having memory lapses).

Looking for something to get many views while practicing your chops on topical subjects? Be the first person to post a parody video relating to a new Apple product.

When the iPhone 4S was released in 2011, the most talked-about feature was Siri, the voice-activated assistant that talked back to you. Berkeley, California, singer-songwriter Jonathan Mann was savvy enough to write a love song to Siri, featuring the iPhone voice talking all the way through the three-minute tune. Within a few days he had a million views. Other Apple topical parodies have centered around the name of the iPad "sounds like a feminine product", new iPods and MacBooks, and mock "revolutionary" and "magical" product introductions by the late Steve Jobs.

Quick Step-by-Step: Creating a Parody

Justin Bieber's "Baby" song has been a huge parody magnet since it originally debuted on YouTube in 2010, attracting almost a billion views since. The song has spawned hundreds of parodies on YouTube—most dealing with songs directed at baby dolls or human babies—and it only escalated in 2011 when a woman filed a paternity suit against the singer.

Figure 2.11
While not necessary for your production, a green screen can be useful for creating a secondary background.

"Baby" features Bieber singing against a backdrop at the Universal Citywalk entertainment facility, cutting to scenes of him approaching a girl at a bowling alley and dancing around the alley's pool table. So there are basically three scenes to copy. Say you want to use "Baby" as a starting point for making a parody. Here's what to do:

1 Find a green screen to sing in front of. Ikea sells a cheap one for $19.95 (it's actually a green "Lusy" blanket). And if you can't find that, check out Tubetape. com—it has loads of affordable green-screen accessories (*Figure 2.11*).

2 If you don't know the lyrics, you might want to acquire a teleprompter to follow along. Do you have an iPhone or, better yet, an iPad? I use a $1.99 teleprompter app called i-Prompt Pro, which mimics a teleprompter. The only snag is that it goes really, really fast, even on the slowest setting. I like to put in lots of paragraph breaks—the more the merrier—to give me time to catch up. For this exercise, put lots of blank space at the beginning so you will have extra time to hit play and run back into place in front of the camera.

3 Acquire music. Start with the music track. Instrumental karaoke versions of hits are easy to find on the web (*Figure 2.12*), and nowhere in more abundance than YouTube. Do a search for, say, "Karaoke Baby, Baby," and you get several possibilities, either a pure instrumental version or, better yet, an instrumental version with the lyrics. You can use this track to back your vocal. (Basically, you're taking someone else's music without paying copyright fees, an issue YouTube handles by slapping ads all over the videos and sharing revenues with the music publisher.)

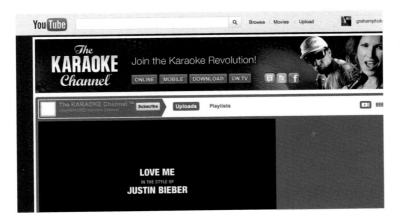

Figure 2.12 Add music to your productions.

Figure 2.13 iJustine gets ready to sing.

4 Convert the video track to an audio MP3. You could slip it into a video-editing program to do this, or use this great, free online resource: http://saveyoutube. com. Just copy and paste the URL into the box, and choose the top setting, Download MP3.

5 Plug a microphone into your computer, open the karoake video in an audio program such as Apple's GarageBand or Audacity for Windows, and record your vocals with your witty rewrite to the track.

6 Position yourself in front of the video camera and line yourself up (*Figure 2.13*). Press play on the recorded vocal track you made in GarageBand or Audacity and lip-sync away. Odds are you'll have a hard time remembering the exact words, so grab the i-Prompt to have the lyrics in front of you.

7 Record your background. The CityWalk shots basically have the camera moving swiftly from left to right. Can you get shots like that at a local shopping mall? A monopod would work great in this situation, giving you a more fluid shot as you go back and forth between left and right.

8 Plan your parody shots. Popping into a bowling alley with a crew on a crowded night would probably cause the owner to ask you to stop filming. Instead, ask for permission to shoot a scene at, say, three in the afternoon on a Tuesday, when it's not busy. Remember, you have a great offer for the owner: You can put up a blurb saying the video was made at Burt's Bowling, and you can trumpet this on your blog, Facebook, and YouTube. Plus, the owner can say the same things in the bowling alley's social media outlets.

9 Improvise parody. If you don't feel like going through channels to get permission, you could try snagging a scene where the hero approaches a young woman (or wherever your story goes) and shoot it on the iPhone. Chances are, a lot of other people in the bowling alley are taking pictures and shooting clips with iPhones anyway, so you could get away with it. Plus, sound won't matter—you're running your recorded song. You're probably not even lip-synching.

10 Edit. The last step is to put your recorded lip sync in front of the left-to-right–moving mall footage, and that will be done in "post"—during the editing process (*Figure 2.14*). You'll also insert the bowling alley scenes at opportune times. (I'll discuss this all in depth in Chapters 8 and 9; for specific step-by-step instructions in Final Cut Pro X, see the last section in Chapter 9.)

Figure 2.14 Replace the green screen in the editing process.

WHERE IDEAS ARE BORN: PRODUCING "TALKING TECH" 125 TIMES A YEAR!

Since part of this chapter is about generating ideas, I thought it would be helpful if I described the process I go through every day to form topic ideas for my two weekly video shows. The "Tech" shows runs twice weekly, and I usually make at least one additional video every other week as well, totaling at least 125 videos yearly.

So where do the ideas come from?

Ideas Pitched to Me

I spend hours cruising websites, reading articles, and living life in pursuit of ideas. By "living life" I mean going to Target and noticing that the giant chain store is now buying back electronics for store credit. Even something like that was suitable material for a "Tech" piece.

Another idea came from when I bought a new flat-panel TV for $800, and was told the least expensive HDMI cable to connect the cable box to the TV was $100—for a cable!—what an outrage. That was worth exploring as well.

I also get contacted by a lot by companies and folks who want to get attention in *USA TODAY*, one of the largest media properties in the world. Sometimes their persistence works—most times it doesn't.

If it were as simple as just answering the phone and emails, and saying yes and no to every pitch that came my way, my life would be super easy.

I do get a ridiculous amount of calls and emails—about 500 a day. After all, how many places can you go to get both an article and an all-talking, visual companion like "Talking Tech"? It's a pretty desirable asset.

These are easy requests to say yes to: Sony seeking to set up a meeting to show me the new A77 camera; Apple offering a sneak peek at the new version of Final Cut Pro software; and teen sensation Selena Gomez wanting to talk about investing in a new app that makes physical postcards.

Most of the emails and calls I get aren't as desirable. Most folks want attention for companies people have never heard of. And most who call about my celebrity version of "Talking Tech"—"Talking Your Tech"—want some press for unknown actors who are desperate for some attention.

While many of the unknowns are worthy of spotlighting—we visited Twitter when it was in its infancy, and saw Facebook when murals had been freshly painted on its old Palo Alto University Avenue walls—my editors prefer bigger names, or in the case of "Talking Tech," topics that make folks want to click to read.

iJUSTINE AND HER ONLINE PARODIES AND VLOGS

Justine Ezarik, known online as iJustine, has several YouTube channels dealing with pop culture and tech. Her most popular video, a spoof of the Black Eyed Peas' "I Gotta Feeling," has received more than 15 million views. It was shot on a $200 Canon point-and-shoot PowerShot with her in front of a $20 Ikea green screen. She walks around with the small camera and points it at herself so effectively that you get the idea she has a dedicated camera-person on staff. Nope, it's all iJustine.

We talked to iJustine about her gear, her idea-making process, and vlogging.

JG: Are you still using the same small PowerShot that you used for the Black Eyed Peas parody video?

IJ: No, I upgraded. I still use it sometimes, but now I have this amazing PowerShot 300HS ($179). It's unbelievable what this little camera will do. It has a nice wide-angle lens, so I can point it to myself and look like I have a staff.

JG: How do you line up yourself in the videos on the camera, since it doesn't have a pop-out LCD screen?

IJ: A lot of it is by trial and error. I try to position myself with enough space in between to fix in editing.

JG: How many videos do you make a week?

IJ: At least one a week on my main iJustine channel, and almost daily for my gaming and iPhone channels. So that's maybe 10 to 12 per week.

JG: How do you brainstorm?

IJ: The hardest part is my main channel, because it's more edited content. I just look for inspiration around me. People say funny things—it becomes a video. Also I get a lot of suggestions from viewers. That's the great thing about YouTube. The feedback is enormous.

JG: How about for parodies?

IJ: You look at the charts and see what's hot. I listen to the radio a lot when I'm driving. A song will come on, and the next thing I know, I can't stop singing it.

JG: *Where do you get the backing music for the parodies?*

IJ: There's a bunch of people on YouTube who will recreate the track for us. We just give them credit.

JG: *What are your favorites?*

IJ: My parodies and the one-take vlogs on my iPhone channel. This is where my fans get a peek at my daily activity. You never know what you're going to capture. I was out in a park, and a remote-control helicopter got stuck in a tree. Some random stranger came by and climbed a tree to get it out. It all happened within six minutes. I got the whole thing on an iPhone and uploaded it right there. All in one take. That was really cool.

JG: *Tips?*

iJ: Just get a MacBook, start using iMovie, and teach yourself the basics of editing. Get comfortable in front of the camera. Do it over and over again. You'll learn from yourself. The best part about being able to edit yourself is that you learn on every video by seeing your mistakes and how to fix them. iMovie is so easy to use, my grandmother sends me video clips she's made on it.

Ideas I Seek Out

The bulk of my ideas come from my own hunting. Let's take a closer look. Here's how I came up with several ideas recently.

Self-publishing ebooks story

I was having a lunch with a friend who was thinking about doing an ebook, and we started talking about the process and what steps were involved. Of course, Amazon.com came up in the discussion. When I returned from lunch, I looked up Amazon's self-help page, and saw that the steps were laid out in black and white. This coincided with the recent news that Apple had just released a free app to create books for the iPad, and a story idea was born. I figured that if I was interested, others would be, too.

Coca-Cola online marketing story

I had a trip in the works to Atlanta, to spend a few days producing some "Tech" videos with WXIA-TV, the station owned by Gannett, which is the parent company of *USA TODAY*. The station promised me production help for my four days—now all I had to do was come up with great meetings. I started by looking at companies dominant in Atlanta—at the top of the list was the Coca-Cola Company, The Home Depot, the Weather Channel, and Turner Broadcasting. All I needed was a tech angle, because these pieces would run on WXIA and *USA TODAY*, and I was going on 11Alive's air as the *USA TODAY* tech guy.

I looked up "Coke" on Facebook and noticed their page had an audience of 26 million fans. (It's since grown to over 40 million!) Clearly there was something there. I went on the corporate Coca-Cola website, found a public relations contact, and sent an email asking if we could get together while in Atlanta to discuss how a soft drink that is synonomous with advertising (billboards, those iconic *Life* magazine ads, "American Idol") was reaching an all-new audience online. After some give and take, Coca-Cola opened its doors and we got a great piece, an interview with marketing executive Wendy Clark.

While there, we also met with the Weather Channel, which has one of the most popular mobile apps and is poised to become larger on mobile devices than it is on TV. I reached out by sending an email to the company and telling them about my upcoming trip. For "Talking Your Tech," "Family Feud" host Steve Harvey, who lives in Atlanta and hosts a morning radio show there, met us at his studio and talked about how the iPhone had changed his life. I got to Harvey simply by looking for the contact section of his website and sending an email.

Figure 2.15
We filmed the entire setup and tear-down of a continuous-source lighting system to showcase the portability.

Westcott Spiderlites story

Prominent bloggers Scott Kelby and Terry White often tout the Westcott Spiderlites, a continuous-source lighting system that they like for photo portraits and video shoots. I could tell from their videos the units looked great—but how mobile are they? How long does it take to set them up? So I wrote to Westcott and asked for a review unit. They sent it, and we shot a video showing the entire setup and tear-down process (*Figure 2.15*). Then we sped up the whole thing and added a voiceover. Granted, Westcott may not return your calls, or be as interested in sending a unit out to a tiny blog, but you never know if you don't ask.

Give It a Try

A place like *USA TODAY* may open the doors, but in each of these cases I went and found the contacts, which are always listed somewhere (even if you have to go through a few rounds to find them). Maybe Coca-Cola won't bother with a small blogger from Jacksonville—but is there a local soda maker that might be more open to a meeting? Everybody has something to sell, and even if you don't think your blog has the biggest audience in the world, the attention is enough to garner a mention in a website's press section. So get in there and give it a try.

5

Watch a short clip of Boedigheimer discussing his brainstorming process in the video at www.peachpit.com/videonation.

Dane Boedigheimer left North Dakota in 2004 for Los Angeles, hoping for a big slice of the entertainment industry. A young filmmaker and animation buff back home, he was able to quickly pick up freelance work for various productions. The turning point came in 2009, when he began churning out self-made videos from his Riverside (Los Angeles suburb) home, starring an animated orange and his fruit pals.

The *Annoying Orange* series went on to become one of YouTube's biggest successes, garnering more than 1 billion viewers in little over two years, cutting deals with JCPenney and Toys "R" Us for a line of Orange plush dolls and signing with TV's Cartoon Network for a spin-off TV show.

YouTube rewards video makers who attract big audiences by giving them a cut of the advertising revenues, which paid off for Boedigheimer, who earned enough for a new house purchase in the heart of Hollywood. Still churning out several "Orange" videos weekly, both for the web and TV, Boedigheimer—who goes by "Daneboe" on YouTube—talked with me about his success and how he brainstorms for "Orange" ideas.

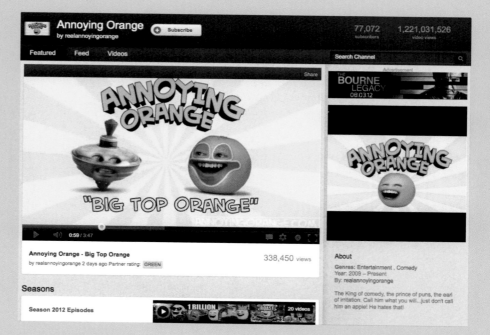

JG: What advice would you have for readers of Video Nation?

DB: First, work your butt off. That is one of the biggest things. There's a misconception... OK, I can make these "Annoying Orange" videos every week and it's three minutes, so it can't take that long. No, it's a 14-to-16-hour-a-day job, easily. You're always working. You always have to try make yourself better and better. Take the things you know and love, and put your own unique spin on them. Watch the local news and see how they edit videos, and incorporate that kind of stuff into your own stuff, and perfect your craft.

JG: What about gear?

DB: You don't need pro equipment to make videos. I started with a crappy $100 camera, a Sony Hi8. I used to edit videos together with two VCRs. I would enter video contests, and that's how I would get new equipment. I would do well in the contest, and then reinvest the winnings into new equipment. A lot of kids get scared: "I don't have Final Cut Pro." No. Every computer nowadays comes with video-editing software. Every iPad, every iPhone... you can buy very cheap software that will edit your videos. You are not limited by your technology, you're only limited by yourself. You just need to go in there and do it.

JG: Tell me about the brainstorming process?

DB: It's a lot of things you experience in life. Taking pop culture references, making spoofs of them. The ideas come from all over the place. Most of the ideas spawned from having weekly meetings. I get on the phone with my writing partner, and we come up with new ideas by spitballing, throwing things out there. What if Orange became a superhero? How would it happen? What would his super power be?

GEAR GUIDE

3

IN THIS CHAPTER, you'll discover you can shoot a great video with $100 gear or less. You'll be surprised to learn that if you've got a point-and-shoot camera and/or an iPhone or other smartphone, you can make a professional-looking video with it. Let me point out some additional tools that go hand in hand with these cameras and can take your production from so-so to great.

It's tempting to use free video-editing programs such as Windows Movie Maker or Apple iMovie. But with them you can't easily do multitrack video and audio—you know, basic B-roll of a basic interview, where you have different shots shown while the subject's voice continues in the background, with enough control to add three or four layers of video on top of the original track. While you can start with something simple such as iMovie, I urge you to upgrade quickly.

Would you spend $50 to $100 to have multitrack editing that lets you produce video pieces that look like what you see on TV? Of course. I thought so, and I'm pleased to give you my ideal selection of software tools to make it happen. But first, I'll guide you through my picks of all the gear you'll need to get started: video cameras, lighting accessories, audio recorders, microphones, and mounting gear. (For my tips on how to use the equipment, see Chapter 4.)

THE RIGHT CAMERA FOR YOU

The first question you need to ask is, do I really need a video camera? In years past, the answer was simple: of course. The advantages are huge: You can shoot for hours, the lenses are very long, and you can zoom in from far away. You can plug your microphone(s) directly into the unit and get the best sound reproduction of any kind of camera. At least that's the case for camcorders in the price range of $1500 and up.

Tape-based video cameras once were the only option for those of us who wanted to shoot sports, school plays, weddings, and interviews (*Figure 3.1*). You inserted the videotape, pressed record, and later had the tedious task of transferring the tape into the computer and editing. But with digital video, that's all changed.

Today's cellphones, smartphones, and point-and-shoot cameras produce good-looking video, and that's where most homemade online video is made. The rules for online video are simple: Make it short, make it fast, and don't be boring.

Figure 3.1 Old video cameras produced tapes that really stacked up. A 16 GB flash drive can store about 4 hours of high-quality HD video.

So, back to the question of whether or not you need a video camera; I would argue a big resounding *no,* you don't need one for your productions. Most budget camcorders offer few manual controls, have lousy indoor image quality, and lack basic necessities like a microphone jack and headphone input. These cameras are very small and have really powerful zooms (positives) but fall apart in low light (a negative). If you opt for one of these models, you should have your subject in good window light or standing outside in the shade.

There is one huge advantage with video cameras: Most of them have nice, big LCD screens that can be flipped around (*Figure 3.2*). This lets you position yourself properly if you're going to be turning the camera on yourself. (Note: We're not "filming" anymore, although we used to. Still, it's such a time-worn phrase associated with film and videomaking, that we're going to continue using it throughout this book. After all, have you ever heard of using the term *videoing?*) OK, but what if you are shooting a school play or sports event, and you really want to have the longer recording time afforded by a video camera? In that case, I'll recommend a few models, although in the budget category the pickins are slim.

NOTE First, a quick caveat. All the pricing in this book is based on early 2012 online findings. Pricing and availability change often, so please take my listings here as a general guide, and don't be surprised to find any of these products at different prices. Unless out of stock, all of the products mentioned in this book can be found on photographer-centric websites such as B&H (bhphotvideo.com) and Adorama (adorama.com).

Entry-Level Video Cameras

There are a few basic, inexpensive cameras that you might consider if you're just getting started. Here are a couple that I recommend.

Canon Vixia HF R20: At around $300, the Vixia gives you 8 GB of internal flash memory—which Canon says is good for three hours of recording—in lousy quality. For best resolution, you get more like 40 minutes. It also has two Secure Digital (SD) slots for extra memory storage. Like all the budget camcorders, this camera doesn't perform well in low light. It does have something most inexpensive camcorders lack: a microphone input, which is vital for improved sound. Its 28x zoom lens will get you close to the action. Like many current camcorders, it records high-definition video in the new AVCHD (Advanced Video Coding High Definition) format for recording and playback. A warning the salesperson often doesn't give is that AVCHD clips don't play back in Windows Media Player or Apple's QuickTime without first processing in a video-editing program.

Sony HDR-CX 190: Sony's $300 video camera records to 8 GB of internal flash memory, has an SD slot for additional memory, a big 25x zoom lens, image stabilization, a mic jack, and a teeny ¼-inch image chip. It also does poor in low light.

I would bypass all consumer video cameras, however, and look to the iPhone or iPod Touch (the iPhone without a phone), a point-and-shoot camera, or a digital single-lens reflex (DSLR) as the video camera of choice for an affordable, easy way to produce videos for the web.

Point-and-Shoot Camcorders

The point-and-shoot category was invented by Pure Digital Technologies, which made the Flip Video camera so popular that networking giant Cisco bought the company for $560 million.

Kodak saw what was going on, and copied the Flip with its PlayTouch line of compact cameras. For reasons that had more to do with corporate politics than the popularity of the category, both Cisco and Kodak left the video business.

Yet the Kodak PlayTouch cameras, at least in early 2012, are still Amazon's video best-sellers and there may be plenty of product available throughout the end of 2012.

I don't want to devote any attention to a camera without a mic jack, but I want to show you how the competition stacks up (*Figure 3.3*), especially since Kodak has now left the camera business. Sony's Bloggie Live HD ($250) has a slot to plug the camera into your HD TV—but has nothing in which to insert an external microphone. Great. So you can watch a so-so video image on a big flat-screen TV with inferior sound—for $250!

Figure 3.3 The Flip and the Bloggie.

If you want a great compact video camera, however, consider the iPhone or iPod Touch (see the "iPhone" section later), as there are many external mics that plug right in. And the video quality on these models—in good light, or with some augmented lighting—is just as good as, if not better than, that of the old Flip or Kodak cameras.

Point-and-Shoot Still Cameras

With these cameras you'll get excellent video quality, poor sound (which you can fix), so-so lighting (also fixable), and a nice zoom lens to boot.

Canon PowerShot 100 HS (*Figure 3.4*): Let's look at what you can get for just over $100: a good 4x wide- to medium-angle telephoto zoom lens, and HD video at 1080p resolution (1080p is a high-definition video mode). There's no mic jack, but as we'll discuss in more detail in the audio section, you can buy a $25 microphone at RadioShack and the $99 Zoom H1 audio recorder and make up the difference with stellar sound.

Let's talk HD a minute. For most web videos, whether you shoot it in 1080p or 720p (the next level down on many cameras) probably won't matter. Just check out most YouTube videos. They are presented in 380p and 480p, and only a handful actually get up to 720p. YouTube actually prefers the lower-res videos because they load faster. If your aim is for the video enthusiast sites such as Vimeo, where 1080p is the norm, then go in that direction.

Figure 3.4 The PowerShot is an extremely affordable video camera that may just suit your needs fine.

My point is that virtually any decent $100-and-up compact camera will do the trick for you. As long as you augment your video with light and sound, you can't go wrong. I like the Canon PowerShots best, but a recent-model Nikon, Sony, Panasonic, or Olympus will do you just fine.

Mirror-less Compact Cameras

These cameras are aimed at point-and-shooters who want to advance to the next step but don't want to lug a hefty SLR around with them. To get a smaller camera body, manufacturers have removed the mirror—which helps the photographer see the results in real time through the viewfinder. Hence, you do all your composing, as on point-and-shoots, through the LCD.

The Olympus and Panasonic cameras have slightly smaller image chips, while Sony's NEX line and Samsung's NX cameras have the same size sensor as that of SLRs. You do get interchangeable lenses, as you do on SLRs, and with them, much sharper images. So your video will be of a much higher quality than with point-and-shoots. You'll also spend a lot more to get there.

My favorite of the bunch is the Sony NEX line, which starts at $549 with a lens for the NEX-C3. The Olympus Pen PL1 starts at $300 with a lens. The Panasonic GH2, which is beloved by many video enthusiasts I know who admire its superior video quality, starts at $1299 with a lens. The Samsung NX-200 is less pricey—around $900 with an 18mm-to-50mm lens—and gets very crisp, sharp video (*Figure 3.5*). Just look out for the tendency of the lens to slip in and out of focus when in autofocus mode.

Figure 3.5 Both the Olympus Pen PL1 and the Samsung NX-200 are great cameras.

Figure 3.6 The iPhone is quickly becoming the go-to camera for a lot of people creating video for the web.

The iPhone

More photos and videos are taken with this beloved Apple device than probably any other camera (*Figure 3.6*). And with good reason—it's always in the pocket, which isn't the case with that big honking Sony you left at home.

Over the years, with so many millions of people turning to their iPhone as their go-to video camera and still camera of choice, Apple has steadily improved the quality of the camera to the point that it clearly rivals those of point-and-shoot still cams. I've had great photo and video results with the iPhone, especially the 4S model, which offers surprisingly sharp images for a tool that initially got thrown in as an add-on. I've even used the iPhone several times on the *USA TODAY* "Talking Tech" videos.

The iPhone camera does have a few negatives: It's hard to hold the unit steady while shooting, sound can be an issue, and the picture quality—when used in less than optimal conditions such as backlight and glaring sun—can be lower than that of a good point-and-shoot.

The iPad

How about a video camera with a built-in 10-inch monitor for instant feedback? One where you can edit your masterpiece on the spot? That's the selling point for the Apple iPad (*Figure 3.7*) as a video camera, with its decent camera and amazing monitor. Holding it can be a little awkward, but look around—lots of folks are doing it, every day.

Figure 3.7 Not only can you shoot video on the iPad but you can edit your video as well.

I brought the iPad 2 with me on a two-week holiday to New Zealand, where I shot five great-looking videos, using the $4.99 iMovie editing app to cut the little productions into presentable, polished videos. It was a little unusual to compose images and record a video with the 10-inch screen, but on the other hand, it was great to view on the huge display as compared to a phone.

For you iPad owners who already have an iPhone, you add both video sources together! Get two angles on a subject, and mix and match in editing, for an even better-looking production. (I cover accessories for the iPhone and the iPad later in this chapter, and I get into the details of video editing in Chapters 8 and 9.)

Digital SLRs

If you think you've noticed that fewer videographers are walking around with heavy video cameras these days, you're not imagining it. With the introduction of the Canon EOS 5D Mark II in 2008, the DSLR revolution was born. With an image sensor more than 20 times the size of the best traditional video camera, for the first time, the video shooter could get amazingly crisp, sharp, and colorful results that rival video cameras costing tens of thousands of dollars.

The most notable feature: depth of field. With a good, fast lens, you can throw the background out of focus, just like in the movies. And because DSLRs work so well in low light, you can shoot in any kind of light—even practically darkness, for a more-than-acceptable image.

Disadvantages of the DSLR: It's hard to focus while recording video, especially if you're moving around, and doing "run and gun"-type reports that you shoot really quickly. (Autofocus generally won't work once the recording starts—most of us opt for manual focus.) There are workarounds and accessories to make the focusing process easier, however, which I'll discuss in Chapter 9. (New models from Sony, Nikon, and the Canon Rebel T4i do a much better job autofocusing while recording.) Additionally, Canon DSLRs can only record up to 12 minutes at a time.

At the entry level, the Canon Rebel T4i can be yours for around $850 for just the body, which is pricier than similar cameras from competitors (*Figure* 3.8). With improved autofocus over earlier models, however, this is the best Rebel yet. It will shoot high-definition 1080p video that looks fantastic, and unlike previous Rebels, it will continue autofocusing during shooting. If you're new to video, the T4i is probably your best choice of the Canon cameras.

For another $150 or so, you could buy the Canon EOS 60D, which uses the exact same chip and processor, but has better manual controls on the body (*Figure* 3.9). Or you could spring $3499 for the Canon 5D Mark III, which has an even better and bigger image sensor and is the true king of low-light videomaking (*Figure* 3.10). In recent years I've been using these two Canon models for my "Tech" shows (see "My Gear" at the end of this chapter).

Figure 3.8
The Canon Rebel T4i

Figure 3.9
The Canon EOS 60D

Figure 3.10
The Canon 5D Mark III

I'm also a huge fan of Sony's recent cameras, such as the $749 Sony A55 and the $1398 Sony A77. Both have what Sony calls a "translucent" mirror, which basically means that it ditched the traditional mirror for faster and more efficient focusing. Instead of seeing the scene in real time, through the mirror, you look through an electronic viewfinder. For anyone who's shot video before, this will feel very familiar. It's not as clear for composition, but it's good enough. I think Sony has done a tremendous job here.

The benefits of this new technology are huge: You get true autofocus in your video—even once filming has begun—something you don't get with the Canon cameras. And your clips can go for up to 29 minutes. Either of these cameras would make a great video-camera replacement for filming weddings, sports, school plays, and the like.

Wearable Cameras

If you're thinking of adding great motion to your videos by adding a camera to your motorcycle or bike helmet while you're riding, the steering wheel of a race car while driving, or your ski gear as you zoom down a hill, you might take a look at the wearable cameras from GoPro (Figure 3.11) or Contour.

GoPro's best camera, the Hero HD 2, costs $299 and can be mounted to a surfboard, bike, ski helmet—you name it. GoPro even sells special body harnesses for mounting the camera to wear on your chest. The camera yields amazing HD quality and an almost surreal 360-degree ultra-wide-angle view of the world. It could be an acquired taste.

Contour's wearable cameras start at $249, although you can pick them up discounted usually for around $199. Both are great for making B-roll secondary shots.

Figure 3.11
Wearable cameras such as this one by GoPro are being used by everyone from extreme sports enthusiasts to highway patrolmen.

LIGHTING EQUIPMENT

The sad fact of videography is that many people forget a basic of the craft: Your image will always look better with attention to lighting. Lighting can be complicated and ultraexpensive, but it doesn't have to be. Some basic lights go a long way toward improving your video images (see Chapter 6 more details on lighting techniques).

Let's start with where I began as a teenager, when I first started doing photography in New York City, with a basic $6 clamp light from the hardware store (Figure 3.12). Add a lightbulb of your choice, some diffusion paper, and clothespins to attach the paper to the clamp.

Parchment paper—which you can find in any supermarket—is the stuff you use to put on cookie sheets and baking pans. Get two clips or clothespins and fit the paper over the light. The reason for the diffusion is that when you shine undiffused light on a subject, the lighting is too harsh. The diffusion softens the illumination.

To start out, I suggest at least two clamp lights, set at a 45 degree angle. Because the lights are on clamps, you can attach them to anything—a chair, a cabinet, a tall bicycle. The key is to experiment and have fun.

Figure 3.12 Lighting doesn't get much more basic than these $6 clamp lights. They work great for lighting your subject, with some diffusion added.

Figure 3.13 Set the white balance on the camera to tungsten when lighting the subject.

One note: your lights will probably be balanced for tungsten light, which is the normal—and bluer—setting for most lightbulbs, while the camera's white balance is set to daylight. If your camera has a white balance setting, you'll want to switch to tungsten. Otherwise, your image will have a blueish cast. If your camera doesn't have the white balance setting (*Figure 3.13*)—well, I'd rather have the blue than shots in the dark. And you might be able to fix the color in the video editing, with software, via the white balance settings.

One Step Beyond Entry Level

After a while, the clamps will frustrate you. You'll want a more efficient way to place the lights so you have more control over where you place them. You'll need to spring for a light stand. New York's Adorama has a relatively inexpensive $79 kit with a light stand, three 45-watt daylight-balanced fluorescent bulbs, and a white umbrella. If you can afford it, pick up two kits.

Alternatively, look for Westcott's incredibly bargain-priced $129 uLite Two-Light Umbrella Kit. You get two uLites, two 250-watt lamps, two 32-inch umbrellas, two small 6-inch light stands, and two 10-inch reflectors. The advantage of an umbrella is that it will produce even softer light.

On the downside, the Westcott stand is extremely light—don't expect to put something heavy on it—and the illumination is not extremely bright. It could add some zing to an interview, but not much more. For that, you'll have to keep spending!

Midrange

For about $175 you can get the Flashpoint Three-Light Fluorescent Outfit, a kit with three light bulbs, three light stands, two umbrellas, a reflector, and a case. Again, the stands won't be very sturdy, but you'll get more illumination and the ability to slightly shape the light with the umbrellas. For beginners, it's a great deal.

Remember that $125 Westcott uLite kit we just spoke about? For $250 there's a uLite Two-Light Video Lighting Kit (*Figure* 3.14) with stands, two small softboxes—for better diffusion—and a green screen for special effects, to boot.

Figure 3.14 This kit is useful for a quick, easy, and inexpensive set up with a nice, soft light.

Figure 3.15 This small halogen light is a great solution for adding soft lighting.

I use the Lowel Pro-light (*Figure* 3.15), a small, 250-watt quartz halogen light that sells for $128. The light, in conjunction with a shoot-through umbrella, produces soft light that greatly adds to the video. It will never rival the intensity of a big, hot light like a top-of-the-line $1000 Hensel, but it's small, portable, and great to bring to interviews. I also use it for photo sessions, which produces a warm light that I never get with my bigger strobes. I love it.

Keep in mind these halogen lights are very temperamental! If you as much as touch the bulb, it will go out. (Your skin leaves a residue that doesn't agree with the bulb.) So use a cloth when you insert the light.

If you opt for the Lowel light, you will need a sturdy, strong light stand. If it starts to waver, if it senses any motion or something like that—*poof!*—the lamp could go out. So with the Lowel Pro-light, you'll need to invest in a good stand, such as the $70 Impact Air Cushioned Heavy Duty Light Stand, or the more affordable Manfrotto 5001B Nano stand, which sells for under $50.

On-Camera Light

You have many choices for continuous lights that can attach to the top of the camera for shooting in the field—that is, outside a studio. The most economical and best-working one I've found is the Sony HVL-20DW2K2 Video Light, which sells for around $200 with battery and charger. It actually gives you two lights for decent illumination in dark rooms. However, the light can be harsh, so I usually cover it up with a Sto-Fen Omni-Bounce diffuser (around $12), which is usually seen on flash strobes.

Figure 3.16 The Lightpanels MicroPro LED light.

My favorite of the on-camera lights, which is pricey at $400, is the Lightpanels MicroPro LED light (*Figure 3.16*). It gives out lots of nice light without blinding folks, runs all night long on six AA batteries, has a dimmer to adjust the brightness, and—best of all—it doesn't get hot. You can touch it without burning your hand.

AUDIO GEAR

As any good book about videomaking will tell you, if you're going to make a great production, you can forget about the inferior built-in microphone on your camera. Using it is a true sign of a non-pro. The built-in mic will pick up sound from every possible direction, which is why it's so horrendous. (If you choose to ignore my advice and insist on using it, at least have your subject stand as close as possible to the built-in mic, and ask them to speak as loudly as they can without screaming.)

Lavalier Microphones

Most online videos and TV newscasts use the lavalier microphone, the little mic that pins to the lapel of the subject. It's small and out of the way, and a huge advantage is that you don't have to stand in front of the interviewee with a big, honking stick mic waving at them.

Figure 3.17 The Sony UWP-V1 wireless lavalier microphone package comes with a transmitter, portable receiver, and an omnidirectional lavalier microphone.

There are two basic kinds of lav mics—wired and wireless. A wired mic, which plugs directly into your camera or sound recorder, can be picked up for as little as $22. One such mic is the Audio-Technica ATR3350, but this isn't one of the company's high-quality mics. When I started making videos, I didn't want to shell out too much money, so I sprung for Audio-Technica's wireless lav setup (currently around $150), with one mic plus transmitter and receiver packs. I was greatly disappointed with the hiss, interference, and overall scratchy sound. It's the old "you get what you pay for" syndrome.

I soon learned that I had to graduate to the $500 level. First I got the Sennheiser lav kit (which was great, but it got stolen!), then I moved to the Sony UWP-V1/3032 (*Figure 3.17*). If you buy two (one for subject, one for interviewer), it comes with a stick mic that can connect wirelessly—a great setup, but it'll cost you $1100. Most low-end mics have a mini-plug connector, like the one on headphones, while most professional mics use the five-pin XLR connector. But remember that even if you buy a mic with an XLR connector and have a camera with a mini-plug input (*Figure 3.18*), it's not a deal breaker. You can always find an adapter to make it work. Any local camera shop or RadioShack should be able to help you.

Stick Microphones

If you want to play Joe Newscaster and look the part while doing some reporting out in the field, there's always the stick mic (also called the condensor mic). I love a stick mic because you know, when you shove it in front of someone, you're in a really good position to drown out background noise—better than with any other kind of mic. That's why the TV news shows always use them in the field.

Figure 3.18 Here is a Canon 60D with an XLR into miniplug adapter.

You can buy an affordable stick mic for $25 to $250—just get a long enough cord to give you room to move while the camera is rolling. Or look to Sennheiser, Audio-Technica, or Sony for their wireless versions, which work in conjunction with their wireless lav setups.

Mic Flags

I like to use a stick mic when out in the field, first because it gives me authority, and second, with my *USA TODAY* flag atop the mic, it's a people stopper that helps me nab folks to interview (*Figure 3.19*). I'm validated by the stick flag, which is that little square or triangular box with a logo that fits around the mic. You've seen it on all the TV news shows, when the reporter is in the field.

But how can you get such a flag? Do a simple Google search. The appropriately titled micflags.com site popped up when I looked. Micflags will sell you a custom flag—you supply the artwork—for $45 a piece (minimum order of three).

Figure 3.19 A stick flag gets noticed.

Figure 3.20 This shotgun mic works better in a quieter room.

Shotgun Mics

Many folks turn to the small shotgun mic—a mic that generally fits atop the camera—as an alternative to lav mics. With lavs you have to wire up several people at one time, so you might want to use a shotgun mic in a group setting. The shotgun mic looks straight ahead to the voice and, in theory, eliminates much of the background noise. But it doesn't drown out noise as effectively as a lav. Many shotgun mics are relatively cheap ($100 to $200) and fit right into a camera hot shoe mount (the little mounting point on the top of the camera to which you attach a flash unit normally). The Rode VideoMic Pro VMP, for instance, sells for around $200 (*Figure 3.20*). According to the company, it has a "broadcast-quality condenser" that will capture audio directly in front of it, and minimize pickup from the sides and rear. I own the mic, but haven't had the best of luck with it. Sound is not dramatically improved from what I get with my on-camera mic. I would never, ever consider using a cheap shotgun mic like this out in the field for interviews because it would pick up way too much background noise. I might consider it for an interview in a quiet room, or as an adjunct to an interview that's miked with an audio recorder. Finally, inserting the 9-volt battery into the Rode—which should be a simple process—can take quite a lot of effort. It sounds like whining, but give me a simple device that takes two AAs—all readily available and easily snapable—anytime.

Audio Recorders

If you're doing an interview with a subject and want to be in on the action, the lav mic won't be sensitive enough to pick up your voice, even if you're sitting next to the miked subject. Your voice will be muddled, while your next-door neighbor's will sound as crisp as a spring morning.

This begs the question—if you're using the lav mic to record the subject, and it's plugged into an iPhone or a Canon PowerShot, where will *your* sound come from? Most cameras only have one input. (Only multithousand-dollar video cameras have dual-XLR inputs.)

The solution? Do as they do in the movies: Record your sound separately. (How will you take two forms of audio and put them together on the soundtrack? Don't worry—I'll show you how to do that easily in Chapter 9.)

Best Bets for Audio Recording

The $299 Zoom H4N portable digital recorder is the go-to device for most video enthusiasts, including me (*Figure 3.21*). Not only can you plug two microphones directly into the unit, for two-channel sound, it also has two stereo condenser mics built-in, so you have four channels to work with. In that hypothetical back-to-back interview we just spoke about, your subject's audio could be connected directly into the camera, while you are tied to the Zoom recorder. Meanwhile, the additional two mics on the Zoom device could be recording both of you as well, on channel 3 and channel 4, so you get additional coverage. This is always good insurance in case the other channels don't record for some reason.

With the Zoom recorder, the only other accessory you need is an SD memory card to record the audio. Audio files are much smaller than photo files and video files, so your card will go a long way. Still, I recommend using at least a 4 GB card, so you don't have to worry about the card filling up in the middle of recording.

A lower-cost option is the entry-level Zoom H1 audio recorder, which sells for about $99 and has one microphone input. I'd rather have two inputs, but if cost is a concern, at least this way the subject's voice can be recorded into the camera, while the Zoom recorder picks up your voice.

Watch a quick demonstation of this audio recorder in the video at www.peachpit. com/videonation.

Figure 3.21 This Zoom H4N is a portable digital recorder.

CAMERA MOUNTS

For any movie or TV show, this is a given: The camera was not handheld during the production. The camera was clearly mounted to a tripod for steadiness—and your video-capture device should be mounted as well. Even with image stabilization on many current cameras and lenses, nothing beats the sharp results of a tripod. Steady mounts come in all sizes, from tiny tabletop models selling for $30 to super-heavy, super-durable sticks and heads for $1000 and up.

Tripods

For video directors like yourself, a video tripod such as the $250 Manfrotto 055XDB Tripod Outfit with 128RC (3130) Micro Fluid Head is the best bet. The fluid head lets you pan back and forth, and up and down, with ease. But that may be out of your budget. So let's look at tripods for everyone.

Tiny Tripods

The Targus TG-42TT tabletop tripod sells for just $16, but you won't be able to do much with it unless your subject is sitting directly across from you and you have a lot of books to raise it to face level. I'd rather see you pick up the similarly priced Joby GP3 Gorillapod (*Figure 3.22*), which is sturdier and bendable. You could wrap the tripod around a desk or bookshelf, for example, and not have the height issues of the tabletop.

Figure 3.22 This Joby GP3 Gorillapod is great way to stabilize your camera.

Figure 3.23 Use a solid tripod and notice an immediate improvement in your videos.

Basic Tripods

Amazon has dozens of basic tripods at prices in the $20 to $100 range. Any of these will work just fine for your production, provided you're not shooting in windy weather. They're not very strong, and are flimsier than a good, solid tripod. A $40 Dynex tripod will do the trick, but if you want to spring for the Bescor TH-770 High-Performance Tripod, you get a sturdier tripod with a panhead for moving the camera smoothly from left to right during shooting.

Better Tripods

As your needs become more sophisticated, you'll want a tripod with longer legs and one that can drop to the ground for different perspectives on shots (*Figure 3.23*). These tripods tend to come only as sticks—you'll also need to buy the head.

I use Manfrotto tripods, which are good, strong, and reliable. A great addition would be something like the $140 Manfrotto 701HDV Pro Fluid Video Mini Head, to help with panning.

Monopods

If you shoot events and want a more portable camera mount, nothing beats a monopod. This is a tripod with one leg, which you hold steady with your skills as a cameraperson.

The monopod is not totally steady like a tripod, but it's a marked improvement over going handheld. A basic monopod, such as the Manfrotto 680B, sells for around $65 and will let you move more rapidly around your shooting area (*Figure 3.24*).

If you have the budget and don't mind paying, my favorite monopod of all time (and a must-have of all my productions) is Manfrotto's 561BHDV-1 Fluid Video Monopod for $279. You get the best of both worlds: a one-leg steady machine that can get you around efficiently and a video fluid head on top for panning and tilting. There are three tiny legs on the bottom of the monopod, and if you position the unit just right, it will even stand on its own.

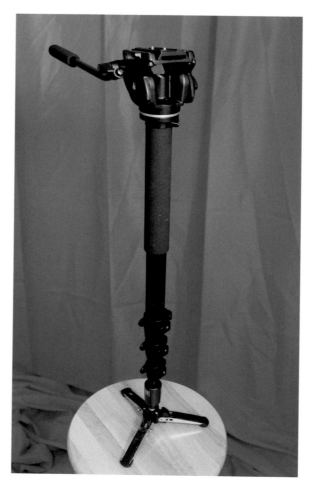

Figure 3.24 Monopods such as this one give you an improved steady rig when you need portability.

Steadicam

You see wedding and event videographers running around with this contraption all the time: the steadicam. It's a stabilizing mount that attaches to your camera with a counterweight that lets you get shots without the shakes (*Figure 3.25*).

Steadicams come in all sizes and flavors. It can take quite a while to get the hang of these units—you have to learn to hold your camera in a new way, so some time and education is required before you start getting great shots.

Figure 3.25 This steadicam is quite stable because it uses a counterweight.

ACCESSORIES FOR THE iPHONE, iPAD, AND iPOD TOUCH

The iPhone is so insanely popular (nearly 200 million sold at the time of publication) that shooting video this way is a terrific option, and will only get much, much better. Due to the huge fan base, tons of really cool mounting and lens attachment accessories have flooded the market for turning the iPhone into something it really wasn't designed for—an almost professional video camera. Here are some of the best accessories:

Stabilizers

You need something to steady your iPhone, a vital step to making the shot look professional.

The Steadicam Smoothee for iPhone 4 is well worth the $150 and the adjustment period. It is lightweight (about 5 pounds) and versatile. The purpose of this stabilizer is so that people can shoot extremely steady shots while moving. Stick an iPhone on top of it and you'll take amazing walking shots—once you master the art of putting your thumb into place for operation. It takes some getting used to, but you can make a marked improvement in your mobile video.

Studio Neat is one of the many vendors selling low-cost tripod mounts you can attach to your iPhone. Its Glif Tripod Mount and Stand for iPhone 4 and 4S is just $20.

The Black Universal Bracket Adapter Mount from Cosmos is even better priced, at just $5.99, and will hold your unit steady. IK Multimedia's $40 iKlip is aimed at musicians who want to mount the iPad onto a mic stand, but it will also work on any light stand.

Action Life Media's Owle mCAMLITE (formerly the Owle Bubo, $160), steadies your hand while you're shooting with the iPhone, almost eliminating the need for a tripod (*Figure 3.26*). It's that good. You also get four inputs for tripods along with a "cold shoe," a mount that lets you plug in an external light. The icing on the cake is an external wide-angle lens, which opens up the point of view and just looks so cool.

PhotoJojo turned a lot of heads in 2011 when it introduced the iPhone DSLR Mount, which for $250 lets you plug your Canon or Nikon lens onto the iPhone for wide angle and ultra-zoom, as well as much sharper pictures (*Figure 3.27*). However, it's really just a novelty item. Once you plug your DSLR lenses into the iPhone, you have a big, honking iPhone that's just as bulky as your DSLR camera, which would produce much sharper images anyway—so why bother?

Figure 3.26 Action Life Media's mCAMLITE (formerly the Owle Bubo) offers excellent stabilization and offers an external wide angle lens.

Figure 3.27 The PhotoJojo is not the most practical setup for the iPhone.

Microphones

The iRig Mic from IK Multimedia ($45) is a little mic gizmo that attaches to the bottom of the iPhone, iPad, and iPod Touch via the 20-pin connecter (*Figure 3.28*). When plugged in, it becomes your camera's default mic for video. Tascam, which makes fine audio recorders, offers the iM2 ($65), a similar external mic for the iPhone, iPad, or iPod Touch. Like the iRig, just plug the mic into the device and you're good to go.

Figure 3.28
The iRig Mic
becomes your
default mic for
video.

Other Attachments

Action Life Media sells connection cables (for less than $30) that let you plug external mics into the iPhone, iPad, or iPod Touch if you already have your own mics.

Remember that first you'll need to go to Settings in your device and turn on Airplane Mode, then plug the mic into the headphone jack to get it to kick in. Otherwise you'll have feedback. (These cables should work equally well on Android and Windows phones. Since there are so many different Android models, give it a try and see if it works with your model.)

TIP If you need to mount a professional microphone with an XLR input, pick up the $60 VeriCorder XLR Adapter Cable.

This one is just for fun: The Olloclip $70 add-on lens slips directly over the iPhone camera to give you fish-eye, wide-angle, and macro views. It brings an ultra-cool look to your projects.

In Chapter 4, we'll go hands-on and I'll show you how you can improve your iPhone videomaking skills.

VIDEO-EDITING SOFTWARE

To complete your masterpiece, you'll need some good video-editing software. Good video editing is what brings all great pieces to life—slicing out the moments you walked away from the camera after turning it on, inserting the B-roll behind the interview, adding graphics and music—the list goes on and on.

The good news is you don't have to pay a fortune for video-editing software. Two commonly used programs—Windows Movie Maker (free download for Windows computers and Apple's iMovie (*Figure 3.29*) are great for basic video editing—cutting a clip and adding titles—but as you get more ambitious, you'll want to move up to a program that offer more options.

Adobe Premiere Elements is my all-around favorite budget video-editing program, the one I usually recommend to friends (*Figure 3.30*). It sells for $99, but I often see it for around $50. You get true multitrack video and audio editing, it works with a variety of video formats (from AVCHD to iPhone and iPad footage), and best of all, it works with a Mac.

There are very, very few budget-level options for the video editor on the Apple platform, in-between iMovie and Final Cut Pro ($299), which is aimed at pros and advanced amateurs. Premiere Elements is the one I'll cover in more detail in Chapter 8.

Figure 3.29 iMovie is a great entry-level editing solution, but take a look at Chapters 8 and 9 for more recommendations.

Figure 3.30 Adobe Premiere Elements is another terrific budget video-editing program.

The best-selling Windows video-editing program, Sony Vegas Movie Studio, has multiple editions ranging from $50 to $195 and is fairly easy to use. With all the different editions, the good news is that for creating video for the web, the entry-level edition will do just fine. All you're missing in the entry-level Vegas program are things such as DVD burning and specialized camera support, which for our purposes are unnecessary. You get up to ten tracks of video and audio editing, titles, graphics—everything you need for great-looking web videos.

If you want to work like the big boys, then at some point you will have to consider Apple Final Cut Pro (see Chapter 9 for details on using Final Cut Pro X). In 2011, Apple made a radical decision to drop the price dramatically, from $999 to $299, and morphed the program from a purely professional application to one that resembles a consumer tool. Still, Final Cut Pro X (the latest version) and Final Cut Pro 7 (the beloved prior version that's still in use in editing houses all over the world) are the go-to programs with the most available plug-ins, and will help you with specialized work such as green-screen and multicamera synching.

The new Final Cut Pro X moves much faster than other programs when working with different kinds of video footage—such as video from an iPhone, a DSLR, and a video camera—all at the same time. In the consumer programs, there would be a bottleneck that would greatly slow you down.

Serious Windows video editors usually graduate to Adobe Premiere Pro ($399) or Sony Vegas Pro 11 ($519).

MY GEAR

Through five years of producing *USA TODAY* "Talking Tech" and "Talking Your Tech" episodes, I've used a variety of gear, starting with an old Sony solid-state hard drive camcorder, and now almost exclusively DSLRs such as the Canon 5D Mark III and Canon 60D. I've also often mixed in footage from Flip cams, point-and-shoot cameras, and iPhones, and I've used new technology such as Skype and Apple FaceTime to interview consumers.

I'm also a working portrait photographer and videographer in the Manhattan Beach, California, area, so I have tons of gear that I use all the time (*Figure 3.31*). And I take virtually all of it with me to every shoot I do, because you never know what you'll need on the job. Here's the complete list:

Watch as the author packs his gear at www.peachpit.com/videonation.

- Bag: Lowepro Pro Roller x300
- Cameras: Canon 5D Mark III, Canon 5D Mark II(2), Canon 60D(2), Canon PowerShot S100, iPhone, iPad
- Video camera: Sony EX-1
- Lenses: Canon EF 24-70mm f/2.8L, Canon EF 50mm f/1.8, Canon 85mm f/1.8, Canon 70–200mm f/2.8L, Canon 28-135mm
- Audio: Four Sony UWPV1/3032 mics, Sony stick mic, Zoom H4N digital audio recorder
- Lighting: Litepanels Micro Pro LED light; three Lowel Pro-lights, Lowel Rifa eXchange softbox kit
- Mounts: Manfrotto tripods, Manfrotto 561BHDV-1 Fluid Video Monopod
- Batteries: Sanyo Eneloop AA rechargeable

In the next chapter, I delve into the nitty-gritty of how to use your gear to make a video for the web.

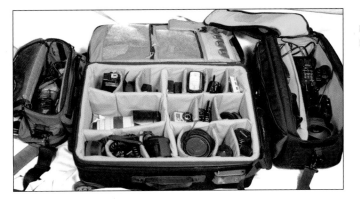

Figure 3.31 The author packs his gear.

HOW TO USE
YOUR GEAR

4

NOW THAT YOU have an idea of your video gear options and what might work for you, you're eager to get started, right? Let's take a quick look at how to use your gear for video—mobile phones and devices, point-and-shoot cameras, video cameras, or digital single-lens reflex (DSLR) cameras. There are a few good apps and some hardware I'll recommend along the way. If you already know the basics about your camera, feel free to skip over this chapter.

THE iPHONE

So you want to use your iPhone as a video camera? No problem, but you'll need an iPhone 4 or iPhone 4S—the two models with the improved camera—and a few dollars to spend for a handful of creative apps that will take your videomaking to the next level.

Here's the iPhone 4S advantage: You get an excellent 8-megapixel camera that rivals any point-and-shoot—and it's always with you. Be sure to shoot in decent light for best results.You'll also want to stabilize the iPhone in some way (see Chapter 3). Whether it's the Owle mCAMLITE or the Studio Neat Glif iPhone Tripod Mount, it doesn't really matter. Just be sure to keep the camera as steady as possible.

Simple Steps for Shooting with the iPhone

Let's go through the basic steps of shooting a video with the iPhone.

1 On your iPhone's home screen, select Settings then turn on Airplane mode (*Figure* 4.1). That way, no one will bother you with a call, text, or status update while you're shooting.

Figure 4.1 Set the iPhone to airplane mode so you won't be interrupted during shooting.

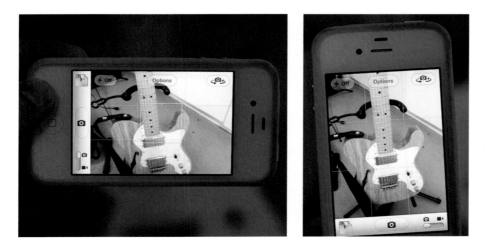

Figure 4.2
Make sure to shoot with your phone in a horizontal position. As you can see, when the iPhone is vertical, the sides of the image are cut off.

2   Open the Camera app on the iPhone. Slide the Camera icon to Movie mode.

3   Hold the camera horizontally. This is crucial. Shooting vertically is one of the biggest mistakes I see. Because the video plays back in a horizontal orientation, you'll lose the sides of your video and have annoying black bars and a teeny image in the middle (*Figure 4.2*).

4   Click the red Record button at the bottom of the screen to start recording video. Click the button again to stop recording.

When shooting, try to keep your hands as steady as possible if you're not using a tripod mount. Also, hold the camera as close as possible to your subject (if you bypassed the microphone option) to do your best to pick up sound.

When the take is finished, the clip will go directly to the Camera Roll area of the iPhone, where photos and videos are stored.

Simple Steps for Shooting with the iPad

Shooting video with the iPad is just as easy:

1   Tap the camera icon on your iPad's home screen.

2   On the bottom-right corner you'll find a toggle. Tap it to switch it to the right, on the video icon.

You'll also see the button that switches between the front, FaceTime camera, and the rear, iSight camera.

Learn how to connect a microphone to the iPhone by watching the video at www.peachpit.com/videonation.

3 In the middle of the right side of the screen (and next to the home button) you'll see the record button. Tap this to start recording. Tap it again to end recording.

4 To watch the video you just recorded, tap the thumbnail in the lower-left corner. You can also find the video in your Camera Roll area.

Apps for the iPhone and iPad

Numerous apps on the market let you tweak the image results from your still or video camera in the iPhone or iPad. There are just as many if not more apps that are available to assist you in your productions. I'll cover just a few of these here.

NOTE All of these applications are also available for the iPod Touch.

Filmic Pro

Watch the video at www.peachpit.com/videonation to discover how to adjust exposure using Filmic Pro

One big drawback of shooting video on the iPhone is that you can't adjust the exposure as you can with a "real" camera. There are no f-stop or shutter-speed settings. That's where Filmic Pro comes in (*Figure 4.3*). With this $3 app, you can tweak exposure slightly, opt for variable frame rates, and get audio-monitoring levels and focus options that you wouldn't have if you just zapped open the Camera app on the iPhone. For the exposure, it will never be as accurate as a camera with f-stops. Instead, you get a selective circle that you place over a section of the image to make it darker or lighter. It's not perfect, but it's better than nothing. Beyond saving the project to the Camera Roll, you also get presets to upload it directly to a variety of sites, including Vimeo, YouTube, Dropbox, and Facebook.

Figure 4.3 The Filmic Pro app for the iPhone is essential for anyone shooting with an iPhone.

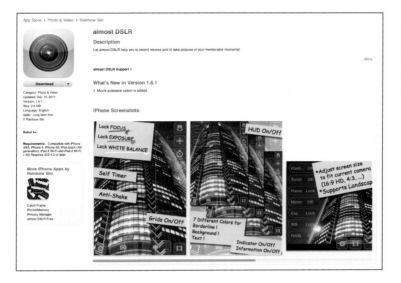

Figure 4.4 Almost DSLR is a great app for locking focus and exposure, setting white balance, adding GPS data to pictures, and much more.

Almost DSLR

As with Filmic Pro, with this $2 app you can adjust and lock focus and exposure, plus tweak white balance, adjust frame rate, and click on a self-timer (*Figure* 4.4). I recommend this app for anyone who has an iPhone and wants to shoot short films.

DollyCam

It's hard to keep any camera steady without a tripod, and the iPhone is no exception. There's no grip to grab onto the device, as you have with a camera, and every twitch and itch shows up loud and shakily clear when you're shooting video. So we welcome the DollyCam app with open arms (*Figure* 4.5). It's not an expensive mount, or a slider to drool over, like the $130 iPhone Mobislider, but for $3, DollyCam turns your iPhone into a steadicam by stabilizing your image, and it does an amazing job. You start off by shooting your video the normal way—trying to keep it as steady as possible—and then, when the take is finished, you process it, which can take a few minutes. Once it's complete—voilà, the video actually looks as if it was shot on a tripod. It's that steady. I love this app.

Figure 4.5 Use the DollyCam app for extra stabilization.

Figure 4.6 The 8mm Vintage Camera app is one of many that gives you an old film look to your videos.

8mm Vintage Camera

For just under $2, you can add many arty and really cool looks to your videos, from rickety 1920s (like an old silent movie) to faded-color 1960s, saturated 1980s, and moody black-and-white noir (*Figure 4.6*). If you use the 8mm Vintage Camera app, be sure to go to Settings in the app and save your processed video in the Camera Roll section, so you'll be able to find it later.

Figure 4.7 Silent Movie Director is another fun app for videomaking.

Silent Movie Director

Similar to 8mm Vintage Camera, this $2 app turns your preexisting videos into vintage productions, with scratchy 1920s and 1930s looks, sepia, and faded color (*Figure 4.7*). If you're a fan of Hollywood's Golden Age, as I am, you'll love this app. A cute image of Charlie Chaplin pops up while you wait for your video to be transformed into something that resembles a relic of yesteryear. A cool speed control icon lets you make your footage really, really fast (think Keystone Kops) or slow. So if you're into these kinds of special effects, Silent Movie is probably the better choice for you than 8mm Vintage Camera. Once you get into the app, you're encouraged to buy more goodies, such as Silent Movie title cards and Silent Movie fonts.

Clapperboard

Big-time movies usually begin their productions with a clapperboard, which gives the sound engineers the sound they need to sync up the audio with the visuals. Should you want to mix iPhone footage with footage from another video source, or shoot one angle and mix it with another, one of these apps—and there are several in the iTunes App Store—will get you that slate and clapper sound. A basic clapperboard can be as inexpensive as $.99. MoveSlate costs more at $24.99 but it has a great interface and is an all-in-one digital slate, clapperboard, shot log, and notepad (*Figure 4.8*).

Figure 4.8 Use a clapperboard on the iPhone to sync up your audio.

iMovie

The iPhone app version of iMovie, Apple's popular video-editing software for computers, has been slimmed down to let you do basic edits on your iPhone and iPad footage. You can also add graphics, titles, and preprogrammed music.

The iMovie app is a must for "run and gun" footage—video that has been shot really quickly—and for doing a zippy edit with titles at the beginning and end, and the app can be used with the iPhone, iPod Touch, or iPad. But be warned: Getting the hang of making precise edits with the app takes some getting used to—you have to pinch the clips with two fingers—and the cuts are nowhere near as smooth as with a mouse.

POINT-AND-SHOOT CAMERAS

One easy reason to explain the immense popularity of point-and-shoot cameras is their simplicity. The models that feature the best ease-of-use have minimal buttons or choices: All you need to do is turn them on, compose your image, and start shooting.

Figure 4.9 If you're using a point-and-shoot camera, get a hefty size memory card for video files, which are huge. I recommend a 16 GB card at the minimum.

Videomaking with point-and-shoot cameras has evolved over the years, from limited ten-second silent clips to low-resolution video with sound, to 720p HD, and now full 1080p HD on many of the top camera models from Canon, Nikon, Sony, and others (for my specific recommendations, see Chapter 3).

Taking videos is insanely simple and pretty uniform on point-and-shoot cameras. Look for either the red record button on the back of the camera and/or the movie camera icon on the mode dial. Either of those will get you going.

One tool you will definitely need is a big fat memory card. At top resolution, video files eat up a lot of memory. I recommend at minimum a 16 GB card (*Figure 4.9*), which will cost you about $30 and give you at least an hour's worth of footage. It's not just more storage that the heftier card gives you—it also lets you shoot longer clips. When buying the card, make sure it's a high-speed card, Class 10 or higher, since you'll need the added oomph to keep up with video files.

The Kodak PlaySport cameras—which stopped production in 2012 but are still easily found in stores—have touch-screen controls, so don't go searching for the red record button, it's not there. Instead, just press play on the back of the camera to start recording. These cameras also have built-in tools to trim clips and share to sites such as YouTube and Facebook.

Unlike the iPhone, the PlaySport and Flip cameras are intended to be used in the vertical position, which won't affect your final video. Once the video is recorded, it will still display horizontally.

Figure 4.10 You'll want to learn how to check and adjust your focus on your DSLR for different effects.

DSLR CAMERAS

For cinema-like results, nothing beats shooting on a digital SLR. The size of the image sensor can be 20 times larger than what's found in a video camera, resulting in a brighter, crisper, and more HD-looking image. Put a beautiful fast lens on the camera at its maximum f-stop—like f/2.0 or f/2.8—and the background goes out of focus for a wonderful image with a dreamy quality (*Figure 4.10*).

However, making videos on DSLRs such as the Canon EOS Rebel line can be a frustrating experience for a beginner, even though the final result can look amazing if you held the camera steady with a tripod and have the hang of how to keep the Rebel T3i or older models in focus. The newest Rebel, the T4i, addresses focus issues, but earlier versions don't stay in focus once you start recording and move your position. It can be a challenge. Here's how to focus with the older Rebel T3i and other DSLRs like it:

1   For the Rebel T3i, start by clicking the movie button on the back of the camera by the red dot. This sets the 3-inch LCD viewfinder to "live view."

2   You'll be composing directly on the LCD, which can be tough if you're outside in bright sun. If this is an issue, pick up an LCD shade, which could be found at any camera shop.

3   I usually set the lens to manual focus (on the lens, switch from A to M) because it won't stay in focus automatically. On the Rebel T3i, you set focus by pointing-and-clicking the button on the far right, the one normally used for choosing where your focus dot will go in your composition. This button lets

you magnify the image—for image-composing purposes only—and will give you a much clearer focus check.

4   Once filming begins, be sure to be on your toes. The subject will go out of focus if he or she moves. To prevent this, try to use a medium f-stop setting like f/5.6 or f/8, which will give you more focus latitude. The image will look best at a wide opening such as f/2.8. This gives you a big, blurry background, but the amount of area in focus will be limited.

On several Sony and Nikon DSLRs, along with the Canon Rebel T4i, autofocus will stay in place when you start recording. However, finding the record button is different on these cameras. Sony has the best-marked red record button—it's even labeled *Movie*. For Nikon, there's a little lever next to the red button labeled LV, which stands for "Live View," which indicates the ability to compose directly on the LCD instead of through the viewfinder.

A good tripod is a must while recording videos with DSLRs, whether it is a small camera such as the Rebel T4i or bigger cameras such as the Canon 60D and Canon 5D Mark II—the image will look way too shaky if you try handheld recording.

There are tons of accessories for DSLR cameras, but this one will probably help you more than any other: the Hoodman H-LLP3 HoodLoupe 3.0 Professional 3-inch screen loupe (*Figure 4.11*). Attach it to the LCD, and you'll not only be able to compose in direct sunlight, you'll also be able to fine-tune your focus because the loupe brings the image directly to your eye with 1-to-1 magnification. (Spend another $20 for Hoodman's Cinema Strap and you won't have to hold the loupe over the LCD—it will lock in place.) Hoodman also sells a $25 lens shade that goes directly over the LCD to block the sun.

To learn more about focusing your DSLR camera, watch the video at www.peachpit.com/videonation.

Figure 4.11 The HoodLoupe Pro is a great investment, especially if you are shooting outdoors.

VIDEO CAMERAS

I argued against the need for owning a full-service, legacy video camcorder for our purposes in the previous chapter, but if you already own one or are thinking of buying one, here are some usage tips.

When the Flip cameras were first introduced in 2007, Jonathan Kaplan, the chief executive of Flip-maker Pure Digital, declared that video was an opportunity because over the years, video cameras had become way too complicated with their plethora of buttons. So when Kaplan introduced the Flip, it had but a few: a red record button, a playback button, and fast forward/rewind button. That design was quite revolutionary.

In 2012, video cameras are a shadow of their former selves, and are relegated to the back of the store where they get little attention. But I'll say this for video cameras: They have become simpler to operate!

Take the Panasonic SDR-H100, for example (*Figure 4.12*). This $200 video camera is not littered with buttons. Here's how to use it and most other similar camcorders:

1 Flip out the LCD preview screen to find the empty slot for your SD card. Slip it in.

2 Insert your external microphone into the (poorly identified) A/V slot for sound, which is next to the memory slot.

3 Compose your image on the LCD, and click the red button on the back of the camera to start recording.

4 Press the zoom button atop the camera to get closer to the action.

5 When you're done, click the preview button, also on top of the camera, to play it back. That's it.

Now that we've reviewed how to use your video gear and accessories, it's time to plan for your video production. So turn the page and let's dive in.

Figure 4.12
Video cameras such as this one are still perfectly fine for using in your web productions and are simpler to operate than previous versions.

PREPRODUCTION PLANNING

5

YOU'VE GOT YOUR gear in place, you know how to use it, and now you're ready to go out and make your production. Fantastic! But before you run out the door, think through each step of your production process, and make sure you're amply prepared for the day of your shoot.

You'll want to conceive of your video production on paper ahead of time, deciding how the piece will look and figuring out exactly what you'll need to execute the shoot.

Once you've sketched out your plan, you'll want to review it while asking yourself questions such as these: What could go wrong at any point in the process? What's my plan B? What will I do if I leave something behind that I sorely needed?

I like to have everything figured out before I arrive rather than improvising or troubleshooting on the spot. To help you do just that, in this chapter I will walk you through the essential steps of preproduction planning. Here's how to prepare for shooting a typical video for the web:

- Make arrangements for your shoot
- Visualize your setup
- Plan your camera positions
- Be on the lookout for B-roll
- Plan for potential sound issues
- Think out and write your interview questions
- Make an equipment/packing checklist

PREPLANNING BASICS

Now, I'll take you through a practical exercise to demonstrate how those essential preproduction planning steps would work in a videomaking scenario.

NOTE All these steps will be covered in much greater detail in Chapter 6.

Imagine you're a food blogger, the webmaster of Great Eats! (*Figure* 5.1), and you're going to produce a visual tour of a local restaurant—Cris Bennett's Good Stuff—complete with sound bites from interviewing the owner, servers, and patrons.

Figure 5.1 In this scenario, you'll produce a video blog covering Great Eats!

You'll be using an iPhone or a point-and-shoot camera to create a three-minute video (a web audience won't give you much more time than that).

You'll be working with a locally owned enterprise, because Main Street American merchants are more approachable and likelier to welcome free publicity, especially once you make it clear that you're not selling advertising. (Even a small blog with a few hundred readers is free attention, and you can spread it further by adding links to the blog and posts on Facebook, Twitter, TripAdvisor, Yelp, YouTube, and other sites.)

Now let's get down to the brass tacks of preproduction planning.

Make Arrangements for Your Shoot

You'll need to call the restaurant ahead of time to work out the details—you can't just show up. Keep in mind you have a great bargaining chip with the owner to get in the door, because if you should happen to say something nice about his place in your video, he can pull out that quote (*Best tacos in town*"—Greateats.com) and use it in his ads.

There are several ways to get in touch. You can start by going to the company's website or do a Google search to find a contact name. It's more effective to ask for the person by name than to ask for the manager or owner. If you can't find a name, call and ask who the owner is and call again later. If the owner is nowhere to be found, you can leave a message and wait to hear back in a day or two, or you can ask for the owner's cell phone number. You could also try to reach the owner via email—the address should be listed on the company website.

One of these ways should pay off with a returned call, text, or email within a reasonable time period.

Plan to Arrive Early

Part of making arrangements is ensuring an early arrival for yourself and all those involved in your video production.

Let's assume you made your best pitch to the owner to let you come in and shoot, and he readily agreed. Congratulations! Now he asks, "What time do you want to be here?" Your inclination is to say the middle of the day, to give you time to wake up, have coffee, and arrive at a reasonable time.

But that's not the way to do it at a restaurant. As the day evolves, there will be more and more people all over the place, potentially getting into your shot and adding noise to your footage (*Figure 5.2*).

Figure 5.2 It's a good idea to visit the location when there are fewer people and distractions, especially if you are planning to interview the owner of the business.

You want a clean shot without any distractions (waiters scurrying about, customers lining up) in the background, so you ask what time the restaurant opens, and you plan to arrive then. Fewer people will be around in the early morning hours of 6 a.m. or 7 a.m., for example. You want to pick a time that's both convenient for the person you're interviewing and that works well for your shoot.

The owner will want to know how long you plan on being at the restaurant. You should be able to get in and out in 30 minutes to an hour at the most to make a three-minute video

Visualize Your Setup

As we discussed in Chapter 2, be sure to think through the story in advance so there will be no surprises when you arrive. It's going to be you, your camera, and some sort of mount—preferably a tripod—early in the morning, talking to the owner, servers, and patrons. Because this is a local story, run over to the restaurant and check out the lighting ahead of time at the exact time of day you plan on shooting. At a restaurant, odds are high there are big picture windows that will let in early-morning light, which should make your iPhone or point-and-shoot production easier than most other kinds. An office interview with dreary overhead lighting is a nightmare—but not here, at Cris Bennett's Good Stuff in always-sunny Redondo Beach.

Plan Your Camera Positions

Before production day, you should know where you'd like your subject to sit for the interview as well as where you plan to be in the video (if at all). Because this is a local shoot, stop by ahead of time and scope it out, so you know what you're dealing with. This will greatly help you visualize your story before the camera starts to roll.

Make an Equipment Checklist

Here's a packing list of all the gear you'll need for the big day. Be sure to check through this before you head out the door.

√ Camera: Is it charged (*Figure* 5.3)? Do you have a spare battery for the point-and-shoot? Don't forget to bring your charger cables and/or charging device along with you.

√ Microphone: Make sure it has a fresh battery. Better, bring two batteries.

√ Tripod, monopod, and/or steadicam.

√ Light accessories: Never leave home without some form of lighting.

√ Audio recorder: Bring this if there's no input for a mic on your camera.

Figure 5.3 Even something as simple as an iPhone losing its battery power could mess up your entire video shoot.

Decide Where to Place Your Subject

Lighting is a key factor in choosing the best place to film your subject. The restaurant might have a great counter where you'd like your subject to sit, but if his back is to the window (I've never seen a counter facing a window), you won't be able to see him at all: The image will be blown out by the bright illumination of the window, which your camera will be exposing for (Figure 5.4). You can add an LED light and it will help a bit, but the light from a window can still be a problem (Figure 5.5).

Figure 5.4 Good Stuff owner Cris Bennett is photographed with his back to the window at the counter, causing the image to be blown out.

Figure 5.5 Here Bennett is helped with an on-camera LED light, but it's still not strong enough to compensate for the backlight of the window.

Figure 5.6 Bennett is moved away from the window and shot in natural light.

Figure 5.7 The best of the bunch: Bennett is away from the window and augmented with the on-camera LED light.

My advice is to move your subject to face the window light. This soft, even light is the best, and he'll look great (*Figure 5.6*). Another option is to use a small video light that you can hold up while shooting (*Figure 5.7*).

Alternatively, if your point-and-shoot camera doesn't have a hot-shoe attachment to afix a light to the top (most don't), you could buy some gaffer tape and tape the light to the camera, or spend $30 for a light stand, and stick it on there. For better options, you'll have to pay upwards of $200; for details on an array of lighting products, see the "Lighting Equipment" section in Chapter 3.

To learn more about lighting the interview, watch the video at www.peachpit.com/videonation.

Another idea is to use the tiny Joby GP3 Gorillapod tripod of sorts, which bends and can be attached to a wall or even a counter. Place the light high enough so that it's not underneath your subject as that would produce Frankenstein-like spooky shadows under his chin.

Decide If You'll Do a Stand-Up Shot

If you want to introduce your video by putting yourself into the first frame, saying something like, "Hey, this is [*your name*] from Great Eats, here at Good Stuff in Redondo Beach, where folks are always lined out the door to get in. We arrived early to learn the secret of its success." This would be called a *stand-up* shot, one of the oldest broadcasting techniques in the business. You, as the reporter, open the video, then move on to let the owner, customers, and servers do the talking, and then you close the video.

So if you want to do a stand-up shot, figure out where it will be: outside the restaurant, at your booth, looking up at the camera, or in the middle of the restaurant with servers whizzing by? Then figure out what you'll say.

How will you frame yourself with the iPhone or a point-and-shoot? Because there's no preview screen that flips around for you to compose the image, you'll need to ask someone at the restaurant to help you. You know how you want the shot to look, so it's best to ask someone to stand in your spot in front of the camera and double for you while you frame the shot.

Be Ready to Do B-roll

The interviews are great, but it's the visuals that will make this story. To complement the static interview, you'll want to have close-ups of patrons eating, servers moving across the floor with plates (remember, video is about motion), and food being prepared in the kitchen and served to the customers as seen pictured here.

Watch any good TV story, and you'll see that the visuals are usually 80 percent of the piece; the actual interview is on the screen for the least amount of time. Your job as a videomaker is to tell a visual story.

So make sure you ask the owner to let you into the kitchen to see the cooks doing their thing, chopping up vegetables, slicing meat, cracking open eggs—to capture as many "you are there" moments as you can come up with. Because once you're editing the piece, it will be too late to grab new footage. Better to have too much material than not enough.

Maybe a stand-up shot isn't what you're after—they're really hard to do by yourself, after all. Think about whether this piece might work better with a voiceover, narrating over the B-roll, in classic storytelling style. If you figure this out in advance, you'll have a better idea of what shots you want when you're behind the camera—and how much B-roll you'll need to illustrate your narration. If you're going to add B-roll, write out a sample line or two that you will use, and then envision what shots will go over it.

For instance, let's say this is your opening line: "When it comes to fish tacos, one of my all-time favorite places is Good Stuff in Redondo Beach. So I decided to come by and learn more about what makes the fish tacos here so great."

For B-roll, I'd want to see several things: the Good Stuff sign; me entering the restaurant, shaking hands with the owner; fish tacos on a plate; fish tacos being served; a happy customer biting into a fish taco; and fish tacos being assembled in the kitchen.

That's six shots for one sentence. Had I not written out that sentence, I might not have realized all the shots I wanted, until I was editing.

So you can see why planning really pays off.

(And, by the way, those six shots are all ones you could easily do by yourself. Even if you can't be behind the camera, you could mount it to a tripod, press record, and get video of you walking in the Good Stuff front door.

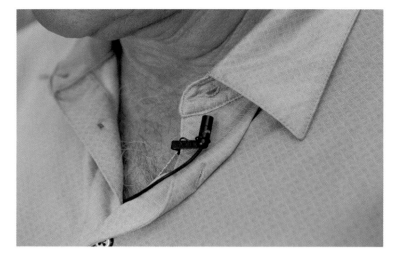

Figure 5.8 A lavalier mic is great for getting good sound because it rests so closely to the subject's mouth.

Prepare for Sound

For optimum sound in a public venue, use a handheld mic or a lavalier mic on your subject's lapel (*Figure* 5.8). You've got tons of competition in a loud restaurant—with clanking plates, the hum of the patrons, music on the speakers, and so on—so you really need a good microphone to isolate the sound. If you must do the shoot without a mic—and I warn you, this is not advised—find the quietest area of the restaurant you can (one with decent light, of course), and stick the camera right in front of the owner, so the on-board mic is as close to his mouth as it can be.

Costs for a mic range from medium to insanely expensive, but there are several lower-cost options, such as wired mics from RadioShack that start at $25. They're not as good as others, but they will be mountains better than doing without. The iPhone or iPod Touch are the most popular pocket cameras with a microphone input, so they're the recommended devices here. You can use one of the mic adapters I mentioned in Chapter 3, or pick up any microphone and insert it into a headphone to a 3.5mm connection cable. Don't forget to turn on Airplane mode to attach to a mic if you're using an iPhone. Another option is the IK Multimedia iRig Mic Cast (covered in Chapter 3), which attaches directly to the iPhone and will dramatically improve the sound. Just make sure to have it close to your subject.

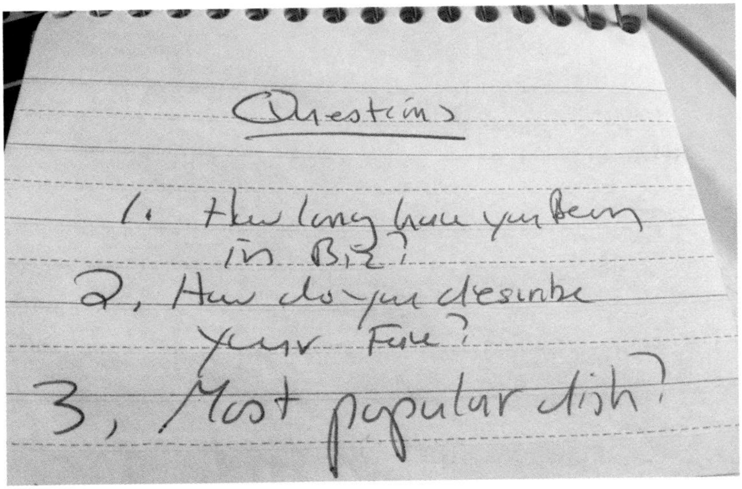

Figure 5.9 Simply jot down whatever comes to mind about the subject and what people might want to know.

Write Out Your Interview Questions

You'll recall from Chapter 2 that another planning essential is thinking ahead about what you will ask your interview subject—for this scenario, the restaurant owner and patrons. What do you want to know about the establishment? Start with the basic questions that would come up in any conversation, and go from there. The obvious works best (*Figure 5.9*).

Questions for the owner:

- How long has this restaurant been in business, and how long have you owned it?
- How would you describe your fare?
- What's your most popular dish?
- How much steak, fish, and chicken do you have to bring in every day to serve all the folks who come here?
- What celebrities have dined here?
- Why do you think your restaurant is so popular?
- Describe a normal day in the life of your restaurant.
- As the owner, what exactly do you do? How do you keep the operation going?

Questions for patrons:

- Are you a regular?
- What brings you back again and again?
- What's your favorite dish here?

Questions for servers:

- What's the most enjoyable part of the job?
- How do you learn how to hold so many plates and not break them?
- How many plates do you break daily?
- What's the worst mishap you've ever had here?
- What's your favorite kind of customer?

THE IMPORTANCE OF PLANNING: LESSONS LEARNED

Go behind the scenes on the J.B. Smoove video shoot at www.peachpit.com/videonation.

We've just discussed how to prepare for an interview with questions. We've looked at the gear you'll need. We also reviewed planning and shot lists.

Here's a case where I did indeed plan ahead—just not well enough.

The shoot was with comedian J. B. Smoove, the Los Angeles–based funnyman best known for playing Larry David's friend and occasional roommate, Leon, on HBO's "Curb Your Enthusiasm" (*Figure* 5.10). He has a website, theruckus.com, that spotlights comedy videos. I'm a huge fan of "Curb" and love Smoove's work on the show, so I thought he'd be a fantastic interview.

I found the contact for his manager on theruckus.com, and he agreed to the interview, saying I should meet his client at the Woodland Hills Marriott.

"Will they let us shoot there?" I asked in an e-mail.

I never got an answer to that question, just a confirmation of date and time. I asked again about the Marriott—I was trying to plan ahead—in a second e-mail—but again didn't get a response, only Smoove's cellphone number.

I should have picked up the phone and called the Marriott, but alas, I got busy on other things and never got around to it by the time the big day arrived.

Figure 5.10
J.B. Smoove
from "Curb Your
Enthusiasm."

When my video assistant, Sean, and I arrived at the Marriott, Smoove had yet to make an appearance. I called his cell and got voice mail. So we looked around, scoping the hotel for the best location. If we really were going to shoot at the Marriott—which I still thought was questionable—we wanted to be out of the way. We certainly wouldn't shoot in the lobby, where folks would walk in and out of our shot. Nor would we shoot in the restaurant for the same reason. I eyed the patio, right outside the restaurant, as out of the way and quiet.

With no callback yet from Smoove, we started unpacking our gear to set up outside. At that point, as I predicted, a Marriott manager came over, asked what we were doing and when we told him, he asked us to stop. He told us the only way we could shoot at the hotel was to rent a room and do it in there.

We had no budget for that. So how to salvage this?

I looked outside and noticed that the street across the way was in the shade, perfect for photography, with none of those harsh shadows that bright sunlight brings. We could do a walk-and-talk interview down the street, almost like one of those cool scenes in "Curb," with Larry and Leon walking around Brentwood. The only difference was that we would have no scrims over our head to create the ultimate lighting and no boom mic to pick up both of our voices perfectly (and no Larry David). For sound, I'd have to use a stick microphone as the lavs would pick up too much outside noise.

Figure 5.11
Try to have a plan B
and even a plan C
when scouting
locations.

Still, I had a plan. We were going outside and going to make the best of it. That is, until Smoove arrived and worked out an even better alternative. He called a friend of his who owned an auto shop—complete with a cool waiting area—and whisked us over there for the interview (*Figure 5.11*).

The reason I was so leery about believing the Marriott would let us shoot there is that I've been kicked out of too many public places.

Earlier in my career, when I was young and naïve, I would meet people at restaurants, figuring that as long as we were paying the tab, we could shoot there. Oh no.

One interview with an executive from software giant Adobe was at a fancy Manhattan Beach restaurant, where we pulled out two lights and a tripod in the middle of the establishment and started recording the video. We got ten minutes into the interview when we were ordered to stop shooting immediately by the management. My save, and it wasn't fantastic, was to take the subject outside and finish the interview on the street corner.

When I started editing the piece, the footage from the restaurant looked utterly fantastic—and the stuff on the street corner really crappy. So my solution was to use some of his street corner audio sound bites with B-roll visuals of the product. It wasn't perfect, but I wasn't going to give up the first ten minutes of footage. It looked too good.

Those are two examples of human screwups—poor planning.

The point is, once you're out and about, something will inevitably go wrong—so you need to have a constant plan B running through your head as a potential save.

SOME OTHER NOTABLE PRODUCTION ERRORS

1) I was in San Francisco without my usual collection of gear—I had a slimmed down version instead—to visit video game maker Zynga to check out its cool new offices for a piece. I strutted in with a lot—mutiple cameras, tripods and microphones, and my three-light Lowel Pro kit. Everything, that is, but my essential little Litepanels LED light that goes above the camera hot shoe. Once we started the interview, we realized we were running and gunning—it was to be a tour, and we'd be moving constantly. So there was no way to set up our lights. Enter plan B—get the subject facing the window light whenever possible, use lots of B-roll and crank up the ISO settings (light sensitivity) on the Canon 5D Mark II.

2) I arrived to a shoot at a department store with a mic cable that worked perfectly at home in a test, but it malfunctioned at Target once I started recording. The save was to shove the camera and on-board mic in the subjects, face for the sound—which wasn't optimum, but better than nothing. And I used mostly B-roll and narration for the piece.

3) We tested a new camera at an interview with two contestants from "Dancing with the Stars." My video assistant thought he was recording—but, it turns out, he pressed the wrong button. Luckily, he caught the error before we left—and I had to sheepishly ask the dancers if we could do the interview over again.

PRODUCTION DAY

6

WE'VE COVERED WHAT kind of gear to buy, how to use it, and how to plan for the big event. Now here it is—production day at last.

The process and requirements of a video production are the same whether you're creating an interview for an online newspaper, a promotional video for a company website, a parody for YouTube, or a vlog for your blog. The techniques I describe in this chapter—how to work with sound, lighting, camera positioning, and so on—apply to any kind of video for the web.

GETTING STARTED ON LOCATION

So let's assume you've prepared well: You've decided to do a basic video, using just one camera. You've charged up the batteries and packed all your gear according to your shooting plan. You've chosen a location that shows action and color, a place that demonstrates to the viewer where you are. If you're doing an interview, you've created a list of questions; and if you need assistance, you've arranged for it.

Now, you arrive at the location—early, of course, with plenty of time to set up. When you get there, select a setting for the subject that looks good: a place that's (potentially) well lit and colorful, a place that shows you are meeting with the person in his or her habitat. Here are three examples from my experiences:

- **Stage backdrop:** I interviewed young actress Gabrielle McClinton, who was appearing in a touring stage show of "American Idiot" at a Los Angeles theater, and we used the stage as the "you are there" backdrop.

- **Owner's food truck:** I was about to bring viewers into the Toasty Melts grilled cheese truck for a chat about how it lets customers pay for meals with their cellphones. So I started by setting the scene in front of the truck.

- **Retail store:** I stopped by a local shopping mall to talk to customers about Apple's latest iPad. What better setup than in front of the Apple Store.

For a corporate video, try to avoid shooting in a conference room, which is where the interview subjects will no doubt want to bring you. It will look really bland (*Figure 6.1*).

Once you've figured out where to shoot, you will take care of camera placement and lighting, which go hand in hand. Then, you will check sound.

Figure 6.1 Boardroom shots never look very appealing, do they?

Figure 6.2 Be creative when placing your camera. This interview with Uggie from *The Artist* showed off the dog's human traits.

CAMERA PLACEMENT

If you're shooting a video with more than one person—whether it be an interview, a small business video, or a tutorial—the challenge of the one-camera shoot is getting everyone into the frame. For an interview, the easy shot—when you're doing everything by yourself—is to put the camera on a tripod and have the subject and interviewer standing or sitting, facing each other. The problem with this setup is that it gets really tedious (really quickly) when all you see is the side of the subject's face. Wouldn't you rather see the subject looking directly at the interviewer, making eye contact? I'm voting for four glorious eyes. For the interview with Uggie, the dog from the movie *The Artist,* I put the camera directly in front of us and moved the chairs so that we could face one another (*Figure 6.2*).

In local TV news, for which one-camera shoots are pretty standard, the camera is focused solely on the subject. The reporter records questions and reactions after the interview is complete. You've seen the result—that dumb shot of the reporter nodding his or her head that gets woven into the piece or the reporter smiling back at the subject. It's always more natural when the questions are asked during the actual interview, so do multicamera shoots when possible. But you may not have that luxury.

Watch as the author sets up the cameras and lights for a shoot in the video at www.peachpit. com/videonation.

Figure 6.3 In this example of a one-camera shoot, the subject faces the interviewer directly, looking into his eyes.

Figure 6.4 Zoom in on your subject for a more intimate shot.

Position Your Subject

Check out two great behind-the-scenes videos with Valerie Bertinelli and Adam Carolla, available at www.peachpit.com/videonation.

I don't care whether you're shooting an interview, a parody, a business advertorial, or a tutorial—camera placement will be your first and most important decision.

Outside shots can look great, but sound can be an issue—car horns beeping, passersby chatting, birds twirping—plus lighting can be problematic if all you have is bright sunlight. Indoor settings usually offer more controlled situations for both lighting and audio.

If you're going to meet a professional at his or her business—doctor, lawyer, accountant, dry cleaner—where should you put your subject? In a chair, on a couch, standing up? If the choice is for sitting directly across from you, try my favorite eye-contact technique: Sit or stand directly across from the subject, and place the camera on a tripod next to you or right over your shoulder. Position the camera so the subject is looking at it—and you—thus producing that much-desired eye contact.

For instance, in *Figure 6.3* I've set up a one-camera shoot, using a Canon PowerShot S95 to interview Reza Hosseini, the owner of Tiffany Dry Cleaners in Manhattan Beach. The camera has a decent zoom. In *Figure 6.4*, I use it, zooming in for a nice tight shot to focus on his face and not just the surroundings. I want to see Hosseini on camera, facing me directly, so we can see his eyes.

CELEBRITY LOCATIONS

When I interviewed actress Valerie Bertinelli on the set of her TV show "Hot in Cleveland," I grabbed two director's chairs so we could face each other (*Figure 6.5*). Sitting on couches can be a problem because you don't get the distance you need to fit both you and your subject in the frame. Instead, you end up with side shots of both faces. We used three cameras: a camera behind Bertinelli facing on me, another camera behind me for the actress, and a third camera wide shot that looked at both of us dead on.

When we interviewed comedian Adam Carolla about his podcast, it just made sense to sit in the same area where he interviews guests. We got around the couch issues because there was room to put our multiple cameras (*Figure 6.6*). For those gearheads out there, a Canon 5D Mark II with a 70–200mm lens was focused on Carolla, and a Canon 60D with 85mm lens was pointed at me. We got a wide shot dead center with a Sony EX1 video camera. You'll notice I'm not sitting directly next to Carolla, but on the adjoining couch, so we appear to be facing each other in the video.

Figure 6.5 Actress Valerie Bertinelli looks relaxed and professional in this setting.

Figure 6.6 Adam Carolla interviews his own guests here, so it seemed like a great place to interview him.

AUDIO CHECK

Many people believe a great video is 50 percent sound. I don't know if I'd go that far, but I've suffered through enough audio problems to tell you that poor sound can ruin an otherwise great video.

By poor sound, I mean hissing, crackles, hums, and other annoying artifacts that come from poor microphone placement or misconnected audio cables. To avoid problems like these, follow these steps.

1 Don't forget the headphones.

Many budding videographers think they can get away with just plugging in the mic and hoping for the best. They might make a quick snippet of a recording, play it back in the camera, and be satisfied. After they get home and play back the video, they realize the mic wasn't plugged in properly and they were actually recording with the dinky on-camera mic. Or that the sound levels weren't as good as they thought they would be, and the audio is distorted. So do as young Julia LeVee did when she made her production at home, and monitor your sound (*Figure 6.7*).

Figure 6.7 You can monitor audio with simple earbuds.

Figure 6.8 Many cameras have a headphone jack you can plug into.

2 Plug the headphones into the headphone jack on the side of the video camera or audio recorder (*Figure 6.8*) and take a listen for yourself.

Make sure there is indeed sound, and that it's at the correct levels. If not, you can adjust them on the audio recorder. If you're going straight to the camera, blow into or tap on the microphone to confirm that you have the external mic plugged in. Know the results before you get home.

If your camera doesn't have a headphone jack, which is true of most point-and-shoot cameras and smartphones, bring a laptop to the set.

3 Make a quick recording, import the snippet to your computer, plug in your headphones there, and take a listen. With luck, the sound will be good enough to proceed.

4 When you put a lavalier microphone on the subject, place it near his or her mouth.

Some people place the mic in the middle of the stomach, but the lav mic belongs on the lapel or the equivalent area. This is a mic that needs to be as close as possible to the mouth for best sound reproduction.

MYSTERY GUITAR MAN (JOE PENNA) ON MAKING VIDEOS

Joe Penna, a.k.a. the Mystery Guitar Man, makes original music-oriented videos for his YouTube channel and posts them every Thursday. From his apartment in Los Angeles, he churns out artistic tour de forces—blowing Mozart from root beer bottle tops; playing Queen's complete "Bohemian Rhapsody" on slide whistle, kazoo, piano, tambourine, and guitar; and performing complex, multipart guitar harmonies super fast by speeding up the video on his "Guitar: Impossible." His channel has attracted more than 317 million views. I recently talked to Penna about how he got started and what keeps him going.

JG: *How did you get started?*

MGM: My first video was when I was in high school when I was 14. I got bored and started playing with a webcam. It was called "Bottle Video." I had some bottles and started flipping them over. About 25 people watched it.

JG: *Enough to encourage you to keep trying.*

MGM: Right. I started getting serious. At first, it was just a hobby, and then it started to be a serious hobby. I graduated from a webcam to a VHS camera that I found in my mom's basement and kept learning more and more about video cameras and editing. Now I have a Canon EOS 7D.

JG: *You produce and star in your videos. How do you compose the shot on a 7D, which is primarily a still camera? How do you see yourself on the other side of the camera?*

MGM: I connect it to a little 7-inch monitor, which I use so I can see myself.

JG: *What about sound?*

MGM: I use a little condensor microphone with a shield on it and connect it to a Zoom audio recorder.

JG: *Tell me about your workflow—the secret of making a living with YouTube videos is bulk, right?*

MGM: It's half how much you make and half how lucky you are. I post one [produced] video a week and usually shoot a vlog as well. The most popular one I produced—"Guitar Impossible"—has had over 14 million views. I was lucky enough to get it featured on the YouTube home page.

JG: *What advice do you have for readers of* Video Nation*?*

MGM: Make sure you're having fun. If you're not, then you're doing it for the wrong reason. The question isn't "How do I get started making money on YouTube?" The question is "How can I make money doing what I love?" Because I'd be doing the YouTube videos whether or not I was getting paid.

JG: *What about gear?*

MGM: Look at the people who got popular. A lot of them are still using webcams from their computer. It's not necessary to do something fancy. I upgraded to the 7D because I'm really into cameras and into learning more about what I can do. It's what interested me.

LIGHTING

The first thing I do when I arrive at any shoot—whether it be for photo or video—is take a look around and scope it out for the best ambient lighting and backdrop. As I've noted, the video should give viewers a "you are there" view while providing the most pleasing, uncluttered backdrop that lets the subject shine.

Once I have an idea where the cameras and subject will be, I get to work on lighting.

Many times you can get away with natural light, but not always. Imagine going to a museum to see great art on the wall that isn't illuminated. Not good. In many cases, for outdoor shoots, you can get away with winging it. But if you're shooting a video about an indoor subject, such as a baker, professor, or bookseller, you need to know about lighting.

In this section, I'll review some simple lighting techniques for your shoot, including portable LED lights that go atop your camera, the one and two ultra-cheap light setups from Home Depot, and entry-level (and low wattage) offerings from Lowel that can go a long way toward dramatically improving your video.

But let's first assume that you *do* arrive without any type of additional lighting. How do you salvage the shoot?

Outdoor Light

When outdoors, look for shade—that flat, shadowless lighting that seems so boring in everyday life. In the shade—as you can see with this shot of my video assistant Sean Fujiwara—the harsh shadows from the morning and afternoon sun are gone. Your subject no longer looks like a racoon with big black circles around his or her eyes—as in this direct sun shot of Sean (*Figure 6.9*). In the shade, there won't be squinting like in direct sun. Shade is your best friend (*Figure 6.10*).

Figure 6.9 This harsh lighting outdoors causes the interviewee to squint.

Figure 6.10 When shooting with the best type of outdoor light—shade—the light on Sean Fujiwara's face is nice and flattering.

Sometimes you can find a patch of shade—say, at the park—but a bright and sunny background can cause the camera sensor to overcompensate and under-expose the overall shot. Or the patch leaves uneven splotches in your shot. I recommend 100 percent shade like you will find under an awning, on the side of the street that's not lit by the sun, or even in a dark alley. The flatter the light, the better—the subject will look great in total shade.

Figure 6.11 In this portrait of Sean Fujiwara, having him face the window light is like having a big, beautiful softbox.

Window Light

Indoors, the ambient alternative is window light. If you can have your subject face the light, you've got the same wonderful flat and even lighting that worked so pleasingly outside (*Figure 6.11*). Photoshop guru Scott Kelby calls window light "the best light ever created," akin to a "big giant softbox" because it's soft, directional illumination.

As we saw in the previous chapter, the trick is positioning your subject correctly to make the window light work for you. You want to see the entire face lit—not just half a face and a shadow (*Figure 6.12*).

As much as possible, position your subject facing the window. Check it out on your camera, and make sure it looks good. With window light, one solution many photographers employ is a reflector that, when pointed toward the light, can fill in some of the shadows. You'll need someone to hold the reflector for you while you are behind the camera.

Figure 6.12 Note the shadow on Fujiwara's face as he turns slightly away from the window.

One-Light and Two-Light Setups

Any photography class will cover how multiple light sources can affect an image and how to go beyond the basics to achieve dramatic looks. An example is the "butterfly" or "loop" pattern, which puts a hint of shadow under the nose and a bit of shadow on the face. Another is the Rembrandt lighting look, which puts part of the face in a slight shadow.

For our purposes, we just want the subject to look decent in a three-minute video, so I suggest skipping those techniques at first and going for the good, even, flat lighting you'll get from shade outdoors or a window indoors.

Once you're ready for the next level of lighting, take a look at what you can do with clamp lights from The Home Depot.

After inserting the lightbulb and plugging it in, find a good, sturdy object (such as a mantle or sturdy chair) to which you'll clamp the light housing. The light should be at your subject's eye level—basically over your shoulder—or you'll get a Frankenstein effect with a deep, deep spooky shadow. As mentioned in Chapter 3, remember to pin a piece of parchment paper over the light to get some diffusion, so your subject doesn't have to squint.

Figure 6.13
Model Heather Syrko poses without lighting in a dark living room.

Figure 6.14
Now we have one light on Heather—see what a huge difference lighting can make?

Watch the video available at www.peachpit.com/videonation for more lighting tips.

With the one-light setup, you'll naturally see a big difference compared to no lighting at all (*Figure 6.13*), but you'll probably see a shadow or two pop up (*Figure 6.14*). Turning on the second light (again with diffusion, please) will soften the shadows and even out the image (*Figure 6.15*). The second light should also be at eye level, over your shoulder. In a perfect world, both lights should be at a 45-degree angle. (This can be a challenge with these clamp lights, which tend to wilt down. Work at it until you get it right.)

Figure 6.15
Here's Heather with two lights on her—see how the background opens up?

Figure 6.16
Finally, here's three lights—the shadows on her face lighten up, and there's more detail on her hair.

If shadows aren't an issue, you can also use the second light on the background to brighten it up if you need it.

Add the third light and all remnants of shadow disappear. The background is well-lit and more definition shows on the hair (*Figure 6.16*). Hence, the third light is usually called the "hair light."

You can employ these same techniques with the simple, low-wattage lighting kits discussed in Chapter 3.

Figure 6.17 A Lowel Pro-light can be the next level for your lighting needs.

Pro-light Setup

Keep in mind there's a problem with the one- and two-light setups: They work fine at home and dramatically improve images for cameras that don't perform well in low light. But cheap Home Depot lighting gear can be hell to travel with. You don't want to arrive at an interview with the local mayor or a chef and have to drag an extension cord all over the floor and find two posts to hold the lights.

If you're willing, however, to spring for two Lowel Pro-lights (about $250, discussed in Chapter 3), sturdy light stands ($30-$45), and two umbrellas (around $35), you'll not only look the part but you won't have to worry about clamping the lights somewhere on the wall. I use the Lowel Pro lights for most of my *USA TODAY* shoots (*Figure 6.17*).

Softboxes

Umbrellas do a great job of softly spreading the light, but you get little say in where the light is going—because it's going everywhere. The softbox provides a more direct light with none of the spill-off experienced with umbrellas. Pros favor softbox lighting because it helps create the softest type of light you can get, approximating window light, and it makes both the subject and background look great.

Watch any network TV newsmagazine interview, and you are guaranteed to see a shot with the reporter and subject sitting down, surrounded by a bunch of softboxes and back lights. You probably won't have the kind of gear TV networks haul around, but you can get portable softboxes and use their technique. The basic setup is usually a softbox on the subject (slightly to the left of the camera) and another softbox (used as an overhead light and to the right) over the reporter and subject.

You'll have to assemble the light stand (which is pretty easy) and the softbox (which can take some getting used to) before turning on the lights. Once they're on, unlike with a flash, what you see is what you get. You can experiment with different lighting positions until you find what's right for you.

An affordable way to get into softbox lighting is with the Rifa eXchange 44, a step up from Lowel Pro-lights, which starts at around $350. (For more information on lighting gear, see Chapter 3 and Chapter 4.) If you're willing to fork over $1000 or so, the serious continuous lighting kits from Photoflex (Starlite) and Westcott (Spiderlite) come with two light/softbox kits.

LED Lights

The LED light, which fits atop the camera hot shoe, is the most efficient and obvious choice for making a run-and-gun video—that is, a production out in the field that has you running in, setting up quickly, and leaving shortly thereafter (Figure 6.18).

All you do is charge up the LED light with fresh batteries, place it atop the camera (or have a friend hold it), turn it on, and your subject now has a nice, even illumination.

OK, with lighting and audio taken care of, now we're ready to set up the cameras. Let's get started!

Figure 6.18
An LED light, such as the one shown here, can be a busy videographer's best friend.

Boua Xiong, a multimedia journalist for KARE 11 TV in Minneapolis, is responsible for shooting her stories, appearing in them, and editing. In other words, she's a true "one-man band," who runs out into the field to get her story and rushes back in time to make the nightly newscasts.

I visited the station recently and watched Xiong at work. She grabbed her Sony EX1 camera, tripod, and lav microphones, and jumped into the news van to drive into downtown Minneapolis to interview a lawyer who was upset with a recent court decision.

After greeting the subject, she seated him in his office, lit him by available window light, and put a lav mic on his lapel. To focus in on her subject, she placed the camera right next to herself and sat below the camera while interviewing him. Then, after capturing a few sound bites, she switched angles, sitting facing him, with the camera showing the back of her head, to signify that the two were having a conversation.

She augmented the piece with a second interview featuring a professor at the University of Minnesota. She interviewed him standing in a hallway, in true run-and-gun style, and then dashed back to the station to cut it together. When it aired, the anchors introduced the story, rolled tape, and then cut to Xiong at the end, where she summarized the story on air and told viewers what the next step would be for the lawyer.

Afterward, I talked with Xiong about the experience of shooting, editing, and anchoring her own pieces to glean tips for web journalists.

JG: As a one-person operation, when you arrive at the interview, how do you go about deciding where it will be done?

BX: I want to set the scene for who the person is. If it's a lawyer, can I get him in his office? If it's a science professor, can we see him in the lab? Where can I go that will bring the viewer into the scene?

JG: Once you've decided on the setting, where will the camera be?

BX: The tripod will always be within an arm's length of me. I'll always be near enough to zoom in and out and change the lighting if I have to. The subject will be in front of me, slightly to the side of the camera. I don't want them to look at the camera, because that's an awkward picture. It doesn't look like they're making eye contact. You always want the piece to look like there are tons of people working on it, and if they look directly at the camera, it won't.

JG: *How do you get yourself into the shot?*

BX: Sometimes you will need cutaway shots. In those instances, if I want a two-shot of us, I'll place the camera behind me and flip the LCD viewfinder to see what's in it. I can turn back and make sure we're in frame and adjust it until we are.

Once the shot is framed the way I would like it to be, I hit record. If I need a different angle, like a wide shot of us, I'll have him stand where he is, and move the camera, with the back of his head in the foreground and me in the back.

JG: *How challenging is it for you to frame the shot without help?*

BX: Without the viewfinder, it would be a challenge—just guesswork. The viewfinder makes it easier.

JG: *Do you ever turn the camera on you, and ask the subject to frame it to get you in the picture?*

BX: No. I feel like, in news, it's my job to put the story together. Ethically, I couldn't do that.

JG: *What advice do you have for* Video Nation *readers?*

BX: Watch TV, see how they get their shots, what techniques they're using, and see how you could implement them on the web.

PRODUCTION EXAMPLES

In this section I'll show you several ways I've set up productions for specific needs. Whether using an iPhone or conducting a remote interview, make sure you keep in mind the main ideas about audio, lighting, and positioning.

Shooting with an iPhone

The worldwide popularity of smartphones—especially the iPhone—has created havoc in camera-land. More and more folks are turning to their smartphones for their everyday still and video chores and leaving often better-performing cameras at home.

Why not? The iPhone 4S, in particular, does a great job. And one is always available—because it's just about the most popular device on the planet. Plus, you can easily obtain anything you need to augment it, including microphones, lights, etc.

I'm certainly expecting many of you *Video Nation* readers to use the techniques explained here with the iPhone. I've shot many of my *USA TODAY* videos with the iPhone, and in good light, the results have been terrific.

Here's how I married an iPhone with a digital SLR for a recent *USA TODAY* video, featuring the folks from the Flipboard iPad app, who came to visit me in my Manhattan Beach garage studio.

Flipboard was originally available only for the iPad. But for this visit, Flipboard was debuting a version for the iPhone, so it just seemed most appropriate to shoot it with—what else?—the iPhone.

I used the iPhone to focus on Mike McCue, the CEO of Flipboard, along with a Sony A77 to show the two of us interacting. I sat Mike on a stool in front of a photographic backdrop and put a wireless microphone on him (*Figure 6.19*).

I opened the blinds to let in some daylight, turned on my LED light, and positioned it to light him. It was too bright, and with the iPhone, there was no way to adjust the exposure on the camera. (I didn't yet know about apps that would do that for me.) So I kept moving the light back until I got it right.

17

Go behind the scenes on the Flipboard shoot and learn more about shooting on the iPhone by watching the video available at www.peachpit.com/videonation.

Figure 6.19 Flipboard CEO Mike McCue gets the one-man band setup.

The iPhone was in a tripod holder on a tripod, and the Sony was on a second tripod to get the shots of Mike showing me the iPhone app. I asked Mike's wife, Marci, to stand behind the A77 and help me out, making sure we all stayed in the frame and in focus.

We began the interview with me directly in front of Mike, visible in the Sony camera frame. Mike looked directly at me, making good eye contact. I asked him the obvious questions—about the new app, what new features he added to Flipboard with this release, and how many people use Flipboard.

After about five minutes, I was more than satisfied with the replies. All I really needed was a minute-and-a-half to two minutes for a quick video showing off the new app.

For some B-roll footage, I yanked the iPhone off the tripod to get shots of the app in action. I stuck the iPhone into an Owle Bubo (now called ALM mCAMlite), a rig described in Chapter 3 that helps you steady the shot. Then I came in close to Mike's iPhone as he flipped pages across the screen.

In editing, I put the piece together, including narration, the B-roll, and video of Flipboard that I pulled from its website. After adding opening and closing credits, I had an (almost) quick one-camera shoot with just a little help, recorded in less than ten minutes that required less than an hour to edit. And it looked great.

Interviewing and Collecting B-roll on Location

Let's say you're doing a video interview at a local bookstore. You're writing for a local blog and want to meet the women who operates the local independent book shop, fighting to stay in business in a recessionary era that's gone digital. You decide they should be either at the counter or in the middle of the store, with books visible everywhere you look.

I dropped by my local bookstore in Manhattan Beach, called {pages}, to illustrate where the owners—Margot Farris, Linda McLoughlin Figel, and Patty Gibson— should be positioned (*Figure 6.20*). I also snapped a bunch of photos at {pages} to show the type of B-roll cutaway shots that would be helpful to give the feeling of being at the bookstore. Naturally, that would include shots of book displays, book-related T-shirts, store signs, people reading, and comfy chairs to relax in (see images on this page). I went ahead and shot the interview using my trusty Canon Rebel T3i (*Figure 6.21*).

TIP How do you interview three people with two microphones and a camera with only one microphone input? Plug the second microphone into an audio recorder and place the mic-less subject between the two partners with mics.

Figure 6.20 The owners of {pages}, a Manhattan Beach, California, bookstore: Margot Farris, Linda McLoughlin Figel, and Patty Gibson.

Figure 6.21 For the {pages} bookstore shoot, I used a Canon Rebel T3i with a Litepanels MicroPro LED light.

Business Videos Shouldn't Be Boring

The advent of YouTube has created a new, free opening for small-business owners to broadcast their videos. Merchants—who have been spending money to reach potential customers via Yellow Pages, school sponsorships, Little League banners, local newspapers, and perhaps even cable TV ads—can now star in and create their own ads to show on YouTube for free.

So let's make a small business video on the cheap!

Assuming we're talking about a straight advertorial—one that updates the old TV approach of the owner talking to the camera for 30 seconds—you can use one camera. If you follow logic (and cliché), you'll have the owner stand in front of his shop, with the sign visible right behind him (*Figure 6.22*). That's your "you are there" moment. If it's a restaurant owner, he's in front of his sign, probably with a plate of food on his arm. If it's a car salesperson, you know where she is—flanked by rows of cars. If it's a cobbler, he's back behind the counter, shoes everywhere. The reason it's a cliché is that it works.

Figure 6.22 Ideally, you can use the business owner's shop, product, or whatever is being featured, in the shot.

There are two ways to do this video. One way is the old, traditional, local-TV, 30-second way. The owner talks to the camera, explaining the deals, lower prices, better selection, superior service, and so on. That's easy. Set the camera on a tripod, press record, and have your subject talk to the camera.

If the online video is just a rehash of the old hard-sell spot, however, I think viewers will be turned off. Wouldn't it be cooler to see Jessie the cobbler showing some of the restored shoes in his shop with a voiceover explaining that old shoes don't have to be thrown away? Then, at the end, we could see Jessie looking into the camera, saying something like, "Times change, but good craftsmanship never goes out of style."

Watch a quick video on applying makeup for you or your subject at www. peachpit.com/ videonation.

Jessie could do the whole thing himself, using his camera to pan the rows of shoes, coming in for close-ups and fun angles. Then, for the closing shot, the camera would be on a tripod, and Jessie would talk directly to it.

For my friend Cris from Good Stuff, we've produced several spots that he's used both on the web and local TV. Recent ones included a basic slide show of his mouthwatering delicacies set to music; another was a comedy video, starring his kids, shot at his home and Redondo Beach restaurant. Both are nice alternatives to the basic, hard-sell, small-business owner saying, "Hi, I'm John, and we have the best prices in town."

Remote Interviews

So you want to do an interview with a subject who is in Portland while you are in Seattle? That can be arranged. Just download the Skype software, which will connect you and others via computer or smartphone and webcam (*Figure 6.23*).

You can also link up via Apple's FaceTime video chat feature (for computer, iPhone, iPod Touch, or iPad video chat) or Google's Hangout section of Google Plus (for computer or smartphone with up to ten people).

The quality of video chat has gotten increasingly better; even local TV stations interview people on Skype all the time. The trick is to make it look natural, knowing that you will add lots of B-roll footage over the voice to make it look decent.

Figure 6.23 Skype is a great way to conduct an interview remotely.

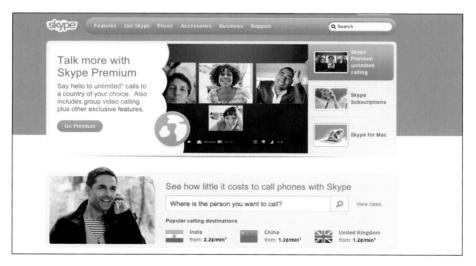

Here's what to do:

1 **Set up a connection:** Download the Skype software (for Mac and Windows) and connect via the built-in webcam in your computer or an accessory. Or use Apple's FaceTime, which works only on Apple computers and mobile devices, to connect with someone else for a video chat.

2 **Set up capture software:** Add screen-capture software to record the Skype or FaceTime chat for later importing into a video-editing program. I like Ambrosia Software's Snapz Pro ($60), but many options are available, including Ecamm's Call Recorder for Skype ($20), Supertintin ($30), and VodBurner for Skype (free).

TIP Make sure the video preferences are set correctly. I edit my videos in full 1080p HD, so I make sure Snapz Pro is tuned that way.

3 **Connect:** If in a Skype setting, contact your subject to connect with him or her online. Make sure the subject's video is on. Also, beg the subject to sit in good lighting or adjust the computer screen (the one with the built-in webcam) so he or she looks good.

With Call Recorder, you have the option of split-screen video as you see on cable TV—no special tools or editing required. Just record away, insert into Final Cut afterward, and both of you are onscreen together. However, you can't adjust the layout of the screen. Both subjects are split evenly. So, with Snapz Pro, I record the subject separately, and then cut a video of myself later. I merge the two video sources in Final Cut, where I can crop and make the final product look better.

You can also do the interview in a Google Hangout, and make it a live broadcast. If you do this, Google records the video automatically and puts the finished product in your YouTube channel. You'll probably want to edit it afterwards, which you do by making it private seconds after it shows up in your channel. You can download the footage and use video editing software to clean it up.

4 **Record:** Start the interview by pressing the record button. After the interview is complete, stop recording and prepare to wait around a while. A ten-minute Snapz interview can take a good 15 minutes to export to your hard drive.

5 **Import the video into your favorite editing program,** and turn this into a nice piece. With some B-roll and narration, you'll almost forget that the Skype interview is lower quality than usual. The trick is to keep the B-roll images moving along, and not to stay focused on the stationary video chat shot for too long.

NOTE One more trick to make the Skype interview more visually interesting is to use a second camera to record yourself asking questions while facing the computer.

Valentina Trevino has been churning out unique "Val's Art Diary" videos since 2008, showcasing the artist at work, creating her paintings, and then offering the finished paintings on her website afterward via auction.

She's not only sold more than 100 paintings at $500 to $1500 apiece, but she's also amassed an audience of 25 million viewers to her YouTube videos along the way—a sizable network that pays off with a big cut of advertising revenues.

The Chicago-based artist makes three videos per week—a fully produced art video along with two "Cookie Break" vlogs in which she turns to the camera and talks about whatever's on her mind.

I spoke to Trevino about the creative process, her gear, and more.

JG: Tell our readers about what you do.

VT: I make an art video, from start to finish, complete with an artist statement and the funny moments during the painting. They all end with a finished painting. I also do "Cookie Break" videos, which are more topical.

JG: How long does it take to make the videos?

VT: I spend a few days on making the painting and one day to make the video, so about four days. For the vlog, it's no longer than an hour.

JG: It's clear from watching that you use green screen for backgrounds and a DSLR for your shot. Correct?

VT: Yes, a green screen and a Canon 7D. I also have a little dolly I use from time to time.

JG: How do you frame yourself on the 7D?

VT: Sometimes I use a mirror to position myself, or I mark the floor, record myself, and see how it looks. Sometimes I miss and have to try again.

JG: So why not just use a video camera with an LCD you could flip around?

VT: The quality isn't good. I'd rather suffer and do it this way. I try to be as self-reliant as I can.

JG: You edit the video in Final Cut Pro?

VT: Final Cut and After Effects (Adobe special effects software).

JG: *What camera did you use before the 7D?*

VT: I started with an old Panasonic video camera—on videotape. It was a nightmare. One week I ended up with 48 hours of footage, and had to transfer all those tapes. I became more savvy about my time and started limiting myself to two tapes per week.

JG: *Tell us about the idea process.*

VT: I wake up in the morning, have a coffee, take a walk outside, start looking around, and look for inspiration. I go online and see if anything motivates me, and take it from there. I listen to radio, go to Google news, read the morning paper. I never paint without inspiration. I paint about sadness, happiness, silly things, envy—basic emotions that drive me.

JG: *What's an example?*

VT: One day I was watching this reality TV show; people were talking about how the grass is greener on the other side. That motivated me to just paint envy and how we always think other people are happier. For "Cookie Break," I see something that gets my attention, grab a camera, and just record.

JG: *What tips do you have for* Video Nation *readers?*

VT: Just start. Do not be afraid of the technology. Technology is our friend. You can figure it out. There are so many videos and tutorials, so many ways to educate yourself. You can start small, as long as you're inspired. What makes you happy as a person, people will find interesting. Whatever you are into, somebody else will be, too.

JG: *Why do three videos a week? That's a lot.*

VT: The more videos you make, the better library you build for yourself.

JG: *And the more potential for YouTube advertising revenues?*

VT: Of course.

SHOOTING TECHNIQUES FOR DIFFERENT CAMERA SETUPS

7

THIS CHAPTER IS for anyone making an online video—whether it be a small business ad, an interview for a blog, or a comedy parody. Whatever the purpose of your video, the essential tips for shooting with one camera, two cameras, and three cameras will apply.

To understand how each shooting scenario works, you'll put yourself in the shoes of a hypothetical blogger who stops by City Hall to interview the local city manager, in his office, about the overpopulation of trees in the blogger's neighborhood.

SHOOTING WITH ONE CAMERA

In this first scenario, in which you will interview a city manager, let's assume you're shooting with an iPhone or iPod Touch. For add-on gear, you've brought a tripod, a video light, and a cable to plug in a microphone.

You meet at City Hall, announce yourself, and wait to be greeted by the city manager, whom we'll call Jerry Humboldt. After you are escorted to his office and exchange pleasantries, you tell Jerry to feel free to check his email or catch up on his phone calls while you set up. You want him to feel comfortable and natural during the interview rather than bombard him with a bunch of questions right off the bat.

Check Lighting

Jerry's office has a big picture window behind his desk. You know from previous chapters that if you shoot with his back to the window, the backlight will ruin your shot. The iPhone will turn him into a silhouette.

The solution is to have Jerry sit on the edge of the desk, facing the window, with his back to the door. This way, you get the most even, softest light—window light—illuminating your shot. You can accentuate it with your video light.

With your back to the window, you set up your tripod at top level because he's at least 5.5 to 6 feet from the floor when sitting on his desk.

Position the Camera

Be sure the iPhone is in horizontal mode (*Figure 7.1*) because, if you shoot vertically, two-thirds of the image will be replaced by big black lines on both sides.

Figure 7.1 When shooting an interview with an iPhone, set it up horizontally.

Figure 7.2 Checking sound first is crucial to your productions.

The iPhone has two camera shooting modes—front-facing (you see what's in front of you through the lens) and back-facing (the lens points back at you). The HD rendition belongs to the front-facing mode.

The advantage of back-facing mode is you can see and compose your image. Opt for this mode, so you can just sit on the desk and look back at the camera, making sure your subject is in the frame and looking as great as you hoped. Then, you can flip it back to front-facing mode when you're ready to start recording in HD mode.

Check Sound

Now, plug the microphone into the iPhone, turn it on, and hit record for a sound check. Saying "1-2-3" into the mic is always good, but the best test is to tap the top of the microphone or blow into it (*Figure 7.2*). By doing this, you'll be able to tell the difference between the on-board mic and your mic. You want to make sure the good mic is indeed plugged in, and that you're not hearing sound from the internal mic. Here's the last step: Put the lav mic on Jerry's lapel.

Frame the Subject

Once you have the audio and lighting kinks ironed out—and you're satisfied with what you believe the shot of Jerry will look like—invite Jerry to take his position for the interview. You frame the shot again, and notice he's taller than you expected. So you need to adjust your tripod.

You've decided that this video will open with a voiceover: "Meet the man who decides whether trees can be removed in Surf City, Jerry Humboldt. The city manager met with us in his office to talk about the controversial tree ordinance in an exclusive interview."

In addition to the interview, you'll need certain B-roll for this section. If Jerry will give you the time, I suggest B-roll of him on the phone, typing an email, reading a report, and walking around City Hall. (You'll also need a shot of the two of you to open your interview, but more on that in a minute.)

Start Shooting

Now you're ready to shoot the interview. To make good eye contact with Jerry while stuck behind the iPhone, either stand right next to the iPhone or have your face above it so he's looking into your eyes—and the camera.

After about five minutes, you're satisfied with his answers. So, now, you want shots of yourself (the interviewer) in there with him. An obvious technique is to just stick yourself into the shot, on the desk with Jerry, but that would be a bore. You'd have the same shot, except with one person, then two.

What I suggest is having Jerry stand up, probably in the same corner (if his office is cramped), and readjust the tripod for the new shot. Leave room on the left or right for you. Flip the camera around and see if you fit. You do? Great.

With only one microphone, however, you will be at a disadvantage. What you need to do is project your voice like the great Broadway legend Ethel Merman, whose booming voice could be heard all the way in the last row. (For our young readers, ask your parents—or grandparents.) Speak loudly, almost to the point of screaming, when asking the one or two questions you want to shoot.

Take Shots for B-roll

Now it's onto filming clips for B-roll. Put Jerry back behind the desk so you can get shots of him talking on the phone, using his computer, and reading over reports. Look for any fun stuff on the wall or desk that you can get a shot of—city proclamations, framed photos with local dignitaries, framed headlines from the local paper.

Take the iPhone and tripod into the City Hall reception area, set it up, and get a shot of the two of you walking into the camera. It sounds hokey, but it works—that's why you see it on the news every night. If Jerry tells you he has no time for these B-roll shots, run around City Hall and capture whatever you can—city seals, signs, staffers working, flags.

Final Pointers

To get around the limits of the one-camera shoot, you can try several things. For example, rather than having an off-camera voice asking all the questions, you can shoot yourself asking a question or two afterward and insert those questions in editing. If you're bold, ask the city manager to get behind the camera and frame you so we can see your face.

You could also move the camera back to pick up a wide shot of the two of you talking—but try to just nod at each other. We don't want to see your lips moving here. This shot will be inserted in editing, and it will look out of sync if the two you of are speaking.

Finally, production day is over. You thank Jerry for his time, and go home to start editing!

SHOOTING WITH TWO CAMERAS

Let's look at how you would interview the city manager with two cameras, even as a one-man band. This is your gear: two tripods, an iPhone, a point-and-shoot camera, and a lavalier mic.

Framing the Subject and Yourself

When shooting with two cameras, I would move Jerry away from the desk altogether. Have him sit in one of the two seats that face his desk. Remember, we want direct eye contact, so we move the two chairs so they're facing each other (*Figure 7.3*).

Figure 7.3 Illustration of a simple two-camera setup.

Put the point-and-shoot camera on a tripod facing the chair at right, positioning it so it's right above where you expect your head to be in the chair at left. Sit in Jerry's seat to frame the shot. Once you're satisfied, do the same thing with the iPhone tripod, focusing on where you will be. Frame yourself in the seat again. Now, ask Jerry to take a seat so you can double-check the framing in both cameras.

This is the toughest assignment for a one-man band. When you're not behind the camera, framing yourself never turns out exactly as you hope, even with lots of practice. It's hard enough to see yourself on a tiny LCD screen 10 feet away—especially since your hands can't reach the camera to adjust it. Workarounds, however, involve monitors to plug into DSLRs that start at hundreds of dollars and creep into the thousands.

So, grin and bear it, and try your best.

Start Shooting

Press record on the point-and-shoot camera and the iPhone, and then take your seat. Remember to project your voice for the audio, and start the interview. (Even though you're sitting right across from him, the lav mic is geared to record just your subject. So you really need to speak loudly.)

Once all your questions are answered, put the point-and-shoot camera behind Jerry's desk. Have the camera face both you and Jerry so you can get shots of the two of you talking. (This wide shot of the two of you is known as a two-shot.) The backlighting won't be an issue now, because you'll be shooting away from it.

The B-roll is the same for a two-camera interview as it is for a one-camera interview (see the previous section).

SHOOTING WITH THREE CAMERAS

A three-camera shoot is ideal because you get nice, separate shots of the subject and interviewer plus a wide shot of the two of you talking. In editing, the wide shot is the one that signals to everyone that an actual conversation is taking place. Using three cameras, you get the most choices and variety in editing and you keep the viewers' attention by shifting back and forth between the three angles.

With three cameras, you really need a helper to run the cameras and check the framing for you. (Try snagging a friend for help.) For the third camera, another point-and-shoot or an iPhone will do just fine—or, even better, a DSLR such as the Canon Rebel T4i or a Canon 60D for better clarity.

Watch the video available at www.peachpit.com/videonation for tips on shooting with one, two, or three cameras.

Framing and Positioning

The two cameras that are facing both of you remain in the same position. Now, if you open the interview by saying, "Thanks for having us here today to Surf City's City Hall, where we're talking with city manager Jerry Humboldt," you can actually cut back and forth between the wide shot and the close-ups of you and Jerry when editing.

So, where do you put the third camera? The only real possibility is in front of Jerry's window. You and Jerry will be in the same seats as for the two-camera setup.

Interesting Angles

Nothing is more boring than watching a talking-head interview that lasts for more than about a minute. This is why, if you study even the worst local TV stories, the camera rarely stays in the same position for more than a few seconds. The camera moves from scene to scene, usually starting with the interview and moving on to different images as the person continues to talk.

So while you're interviewing the city manager, you need to ask yourself, what can I do to illustrate the dialogue? Because the interview is about the tree issues in town, you can go out and get shots of the big trees and the roots that are cracking the sidewalks (*Figure 7.4*). If you're really into it, find a way to climb up a branch or two in order to get a shot from above. Maybe a neighbor will let you shoot out of a second- or third-floor window.

Figure 7.4 Find unique shots to use in your productions.

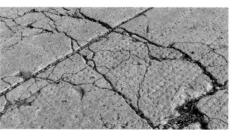

IMPORTANT TIPS

Yes, you're sitting with the city manager and talking local politics, but you need to make sure your visuals are everything they need to be to help tell the story and captivate the viewer. It's better to take the time during the interview rather than be stuck trying to salvage something later.

Avoid an Embarrassing Shoot

Even if you're in a rush and concerned about taking too much of your interview subject's time, it's unwise to just throw the camera on without spending enough time framing the shot. You can end up like me, with a toilet ruining an interview.

A big-time CEO agreed to talk tech with me in Las Vegas for *USA TODAY*. It was late in the day and we had just enough daylight to make the room and the shot look good. Once the camera was in place, the sound checked, and everything ready to go, I visited the bathroom. When I returned, I continued shooting opposite my subject, who was seated on the lavish hotel couch.

Later that night, when checking the footage, I was shocked to discover a shot of my subject with a big white toilet clearly visible in every frame of the video (*Figure 7.5*). I had neglected to close the bathroom door!

Sean, who was shooting for me, didn't see it. I certainly didn't notice it either. But I sure we wish we had taken the time for one more inspection!

Figure 7.5 Recheck your frame to prevent embarassing shots like this one, which features a toilet.

Figure 7.6 If the space allows it, move around to different rooms or to the outside for a change of pace.

Keep Things Moving

In an interview video, I always try to keep it interesting by moving it around, if I can. When we did the piece on Dane Boedigheimer and his YouTube "Annoying Orange" videos, we had the luxury of doing it at his home. I asked a few questions in one setting, then asked if we could shoot in another wing of the house.

We started in the garage, where he makes the videos, then went inside and got him in front of his computer, where he adds the special effects that turn a static orange into a wise-cracking animated creation. We then did a scene in his kitchen, sitting at the table, with two oranges in front of us (*Figure 7.6*).

In the editing, I used one sound bite from each location along with B-roll clips of the "Orange" show and of Boedigheimer recording his script into the camera, juggling some oranges, and showing off an "Orange" mask.

The other night, ABC's "Nightline" ran a piece about movie director James Cameron and his environmentally friendly ranch near Santa Barbara, California. In the seven-minute piece, ABC moved all over the place—just like my little "Tech" videos. The piece included sound bites of Cameron in his home, being interviewed by anchor Bill Weir, driving down the road in his car, and walking out near his solar panels.

Of course, these are the dream pieces. The city manager interview doesn't afford such possibilities. He's not going to take a drive with you in a Chevy Volt to show you the trees. He has to get back to work. But you never know if you don't ask.

Stay on Topic

Let's say you ask a question, and Jerry responds by talking...and talking...and talking. You don't want to be rude and cut him off, but, on the other hand, you can't run this long-winded answer either. What do you do?

Dane Boedigheimer gives his advice on making videos in this video at www.peachpit.com/videonation.

You have no choice but to jump in. You are in control. You are the master of ceremonies here.

Chris Matthews of MSNBC is known for constantly cutting off people as they speak, and it doesn't seem to hurt him. I find the way he interrupts his subjects to be quite obnoxious, but he's still on the air, and he still gets great guests.

Like Matthews, you have to stay on topic and keep things moving. If the interviewee is starting to wander off, just jump in with your on-topic question to bring him or her back.

Wrap It Up

How do you know when it's time to end an interview? In a first video interview, you want only two or three short, interesting sound bites at best. You can achieve this in five to ten minutes at most. Any longer and you can drive yourself crazy going through up to an hour of interview footage to find those one or two minutes of sound-bite material for your piece. Remember, the Internet is short attention-span theater. Most YouTube clips are three minutes or less.

Remember the Five Ws of Interviewing

When framing your questions for the city manager, keep in mind the five Ws: who (locals complaining), what (the tree policy), when (now), where (in the local community), and why (because tree roots are cracking many resident sidewalks). Questions you might come up with include:

- This policy has been in place for many years. Why do you think the issue is heating up now?

- Why can't the policy be amended?

- In these recessionary times, many homeowners don't think they should have to pay thousands of dollars to deal with trees, which they are not allowed to remove from their property. What can they do?

As you conduct the interview, listen to the answers carefully. That way, you'll naturally have questions of your own, just as you would in any normal conversation. So far, this book has covered a lot of material about planning ahead and thinking your questions through. The most important attribute of an interviewer, however, is being a good listener. For a great interview, your questions should be based on the subject's responses.

In early 2012, I met Penn Jillette—the talkative half of the Penn & Teller magic duo—in Las Vegas for a "Talking Your Tech" interview. The show features celebrities chatting about the tech gear they love to use.

I knew that Penn was an avid blogger, vlogger, and Tweeter; e-reader fan; and tech enthusiast going back to the 1980s. He's also, obviously, a skilled magician.

After setting up three cameras backstage at the Rio All-Suite Hotel and Casino in Las Vegas, and getting the sound worked out, we sat down for the interview (*Figure 7.7*).

Penn was surrounded by magic posters and the like, so I began by asking him about technology and magic. He said that live magic is analog—when he swallows fire on stage, it's real flames.

Then, we jumped into his years of geekdom. (He said that he had one of the first email addresses and nearly 2 million followers on Twitter.) But when I said, "You're a big e-reader, I hear," the interview totally came alive.

Penn explained that he used to be a big fan of the Amazon Kindle e-reader—but he had this habit of bringing it into the bathtub to read at night, and he'd end up dropping it into the water.

Figure 7.7
The surroundings in the interview capture the unique personality of Penn Jillette from Penn & Teller.

My ears perked up and I dived right into follow-up mode. We continued on the bath theme, talking about what books he liked to read in the tub (the Bible, of all things, from the prominent atheist) and why the iPad was better for tub reading (because it is bigger and heavier, and less likely to fall).

Penn also described his other current favorite tech gear: headphones by Fanny Wang.

"I just love the name," he said. "Fanny Wang. Who cares about the quality? Having something named Fanny Wang hanging off the side of your bag is pretty great."

So, naturally, I followed up by asking how often he dropped the headphones in the bath. He replied with a cute answer about tying the headphone cord around his hair to make sure they wouldn't fall in. "I'm a real expert at electronics in the bathtub," he added.

This was one of my favorite interviews of the year—with answers I never expected—and follow-up questions that came naturally from listening.

Go behind the scenes with the author and Penn Jillette by watching the video at www.peachpit.com/videonation.

VIDEO EDITING

8

WHEN WRITING, HOSTING, and producing videos, editing is the part I love the most. I find it an absolute thrill to come back from a shoot and turn my raw material into a watchable three minutes of the most popular format known to man: visual storytelling. Let's face it: For decades, most folks have gotten their information from television—because they simply prefer showing and telling to reading.

That same visual storytelling has moved to the web, where people can now look to video to see the sights and sounds of their neighbors, local celebrities, and newsmakers. But for many, video editing seems like a daunting task. The challenge in getting people to edit is reducing the fear, says Larry Jordan, a noted video-editing expert and the author of Peachpit's *Final Cut Pro X: Making the Transition*. "There are all different ways of saying…'I'll get around to it later.' But once you make the commitment to telling your story, and sit down and actually do it, you realize it wasn't that hard after all."

It's in video editing where you get to let out your inner Spielberg. You are the director, producer, and editor. Want a close-up as your first shot, followed by a wide shot? That's your call. You get to decide which shots go where, how to improve them with cropping, and when to add B-roll. You make all the decisions.

At this point in the process, you may have at least an hour of video footage— and you're ready to cut it down to a nice three-minute piece, complete with titles, transitions, and some special effects. All of this takes time, but as you'll see, the effort is well worth it.

ENTRY-LEVEL EDITING PROGRAMS

Most beginners start editing with free software that came with their computer or is widely available. Video editors eventually graduate to full-featured programs for more options and controls.

- **Windows:** Windows users tend to start with Movie Maker, a free download for doing very simple edits, including titles and basic special effects. As they gain experience, they might migrate to Adobe Premiere Elements, Pinnacle Studio, or Sony Vegas.

- **Mac:** Mac users usually start with iMovie, which comes free with newer Macs and is more robust than Movie Maker. Later, they might try Adobe Premiere Elements (*Figure* 8.1). Elements is the only good, consumer-level, non-Apple, video-editing alternative I know of for the Mac, and it's affordable ($99). Besides iMovie, there's also Apple's Final Cut Pro X ($299) and Adobe Premiere Pro ($799) for professionals.

Figure 8.1 Adobe Premiere Elements is a great, consumer-level, video-editing program.

Previously, with its $1000 price tag, Final Cut Pro was aimed at pros and semi-pros itching to make professional-level productions. Now, it's now come down to earth, with a more consumer-friendly interface and an affordable $299 price tag. If you start making more videos, I recommend working your way up to a program such as Adobe Premiere Pro or Final Cut Pro. I use Final Cut Pro, five days a week, to churn out my "Talking Tech" series. It has everything you need to make great-looking videos (see Chapter 9).

Later in this chapter, I provide step-by-step instructions on using software for your projects. For now, let me guide you through the hardware you need to edit video for the web. If you have already selected your hardware and software programs, feel free to skip over these sections.

HARDWARE REQUIRED FOR EDITING

What type of computer do you need to start editing video? To do serious, heavy-duty work, you'll eventually need a machine with lots of processing speed and extra RAM. But to start out, any good entry-level computer on the market will do just fine. Most cameras used for video today—at least the type discussed in this book—use either memory cards or internal flash memory. So you will need a computer with a USB slot or a built-in SD card reader (which many computers have) to transfer your footage (Figure 8.2).

Figure 8.2 An Apple iMac is a great computer for video editing. It's even better with extra RAM, which gives the computer more oomph.

The basic computers recommended here are acceptable for basic video editing. (Note that you may need to pay more for a monitor, keyboard and mouse.) As you advance to multiple cameras, green screen, and lots of graphics, you'll want a machine with more power.

Windows Recommendations

For Windows, a Hewlett-Packard p2-1110 sells for just over $300, has 3 GB of RAM, a 1.65 GHz processor, and—best of all—six USB slots. With computer prices falling all the time, by the time you read this you might find a Windows machine with similar specs for $250 or even lower.

This might not have enough power for serious video editing. If you want to step up, for around $1000, try the HP Omni 220 Quad, with a 2.8 GHz quad-core chip, 8 GB of RAM, and a whopping 1 TB hard drive. If you choose this one, upgrade the RAM to 16 GB so the computer will run much faster.

Mac Recommendations

The current entry-level Mac, the Mac Mini ($559), offers a 2.3 GHz chip, a 500 GB hard drive, and 2 GB of RAM. That's really not enough for heavy-duty video editing. If that's your goal, I suggest the entry-level, 21-inch iMac, with the standard 2.3 GHz chip, 500 GB hard drive, and a boost in RAM to at least 8 GB, for starters. This will run you around $1400. RAM is essential: It's what makes the programs run smoothly and lets you have multiple programs open at once.

Figure 8.3 Good external drives such as these are important for backing up your files.

External Drives

Storing copies of your video files on a secondary hard drive is crucial. I've already lost three drives this year. Two of my pocket USB drives—the cheapest and most prone to crash—bit the dust with no warning. I simply unmounted them from my Mac laptop, put them in a backpack—in a secure, small window—and drove to a computer store. Once I arrived, the drives were toast.

The moral to these stories: Make sure your files are backed up like mine were. Consider an investment of $200 to $300 for two good, reliable, desktop hard drives that plug into the AC for power (*Figure 8.3*). These drives tend to be the most reliable. Still, I wouldn't trust storing the footage on just one drive. Two are essential. That way, if one fails, you always have the other as your backup.

In the last few years, cloud storage has become popular. This means moving your files to the Internet for storage on sites such as Carbonite and Dropbox or photo-specialist sites such as Smugmug and Phanfare.

These cloud services are great for photos, but raw video files are huge and can take hours, if not days, to upload to a service. We usually return from shoots with 15 GB to 20 GB of video. Not only would it be extremely costly to upload 20 GB to a website, it would also take a really long time. That's why most folks look to multiple hard drives to handle their video data.

Figure 8.4 A card reader lets you bypass the battery-draining aspects of plugging the camera directly into the computer.

Card Readers

I use either a card reader (*Figure 8.4*) or the built-in computer SD slot to import my footage. You can plug your camera directly into the computer via a USB cable, but this is not ideal. By plugging the camera in, you're eating away at the battery—and why would you want to do that? It's also a much slower way to bring in the video files.

So get a good card reader—available for as low as $15 at camera stores and your local CVS or Walgreens—or use the slot on the computer.

THE ESSENTIALS OF VIDEO EDITING

No matter what video-editing software you use, the basics of editing are always the same. You turn raw footage into mini-masterpieces by trimming out the excess and leaving in the good stuff. Then, you pretty it up with B-roll to help tell the story visually and add transitions to keep the content flowing.

Whether you're shooting a parody, a small-business video, or an interview for a blog, you will come home with probably five to ten times more material than will make it into the finished piece. A conversation with an interview subject, for example, may be 15 or 20 minutes. Local TV news pieces, however, tend to run only 90 to 120 seconds, tops. On the web, you might expand that to three minutes, but online-viewers' attention spans just won't last much longer. (Newsmagazine pieces like those on "60 Minutes" and "Rock Center" tend to be about 15 minutes long. These pieces use the extra time for better visual storytelling and hot interviews. But let's face it—if you can get the elusive Madonna or Adele to sit down for an interview, it can run as long as you'd like it to be.)

Figure 8.5 You can watch Jefferson's interview with Kermit the Frog on *USA TODAY*'s web site (www.usatoday.com/tech/columnist/talkingyourtech/story/2012-03-18/kermit-talking-tech/53614160/1).

Why are video pieces generally so short? Because the medium calls for to-the-point stories. Tell me what you're trying to say. Get in and get out. As the editor, you will turn the conversation into a story. Even though you go into each shoot with a clear story angle and carefully though-out questions, people may respond differently from the way you imagined. In editing, you'll find the best responses and the best shots, and piece them together artfully.

Toward the end of the editing process, you'll add titles, transitions, and graphics, creating eye candy that's a lot of fun to watch.

Here's an example: One of my all-time favorite *USA TODAY* interviews was with Kermit the Frog, a fun meeting that featured the iconic Muppet talking about his views on subjects near and dear to my target audience: texting, smartphones, and video cameras (*Figure 8.5*).

I ended the interview by pulling out my guitar and playing the "Muppet Show" theme song—and Kermit sang along. I walked out of there on cloud nine, feeling I had reached a career high. A duet with Kermit! A fun romp.

But, when I put the entire interview together on the timeline, it wasn't as much fun as I remembered. It was cute, but kind of rambling, with not enough of Kermit—and way too much of me. That was the first cut, at seven minutes long.

As you will discover when you go out with your cameras, sometimes the best responses are in the middle of the interview, not in the beginning. Sometimes people need a little time to warm up. Maybe the middle will sag and the best stuff is at the tail end. Maybe you initially liked questions 2 and 5, but in the editing, you find they work better in reverse order.

So I got to work, trimming, keeping in just the best parts. Finally, I arrived at a three-minute cut, with the excess available to anyone who wanted to watch as an extended bonus cut.

GETTING STARTED WITH THE EDITING WORKFLOW

Before I begin editing a video, I create and name a folder for the video files. I create the folder in one place on an external drive connected to my computer, and import the video files into that folder. For backup, I immediately copy the folder and its files to a second external hard drive. (See the "External Drives" section earlier in this chapter.) This way I have two sets of files—on two separate drives. I don't store video or photo files on my computer's internal drive because I like to have all my storage in a separate place. Plus, I don't want to muck up the internal drive with hundreds of gigabytes of video footage.

So, let's say you've connected your card reader, USB cable for the iPhone, or iPad to the computer. In addition, you've created a folder for the production, and you're bringing in the footage to the first external drive. In this folder, which we'll review later, you can insert other assets for your video, such as a special title created in Photoshop, additional B-roll images pulled from the web, or a song you want to use on the soundtrack.

The Basic Editing Process

Here's a step-by-step overview of the editing process:

1 Import your footage to the computer.

2 View the material and identify the key moments you want to see in your final production.

3 Move the clips around to tell a coherent story.

4 Once the main clips are in place, add cutaway shots (B-roll) to illustrate what you're trying to say—and make the video more interesting with different camera angles.

5 Add narration, music, titles, transitions, still photos, and graphics.

6 Watch the video to make sure everything looks like it's supposed to. Adjust where needed.

7 Save the final file and export it to the hard drive.

That's the quick version. Following is an amplified version, with a little more color.

Import and View Your Footage

After you import the footage, sit and watch the video to identify the sound bites you like. You can either view it within your video-editing software or on the computer itself. Because I'm a journalist, and I always write an article to go with the video, I transcribe the footage as I'm playing it, stopping and starting the video over and over again to get the transcription right. Then I print out the text, highlight the sound bites, and write a script.

TIP It's hard to type in a word processor such as Microsoft Word while a video is playing in iMovie or Premiere Elements. The video will stop playing. So I open a simple text editor, such as TextEdit on Mac or Notepad on Windows, to get around this.

Create a Script and Record Narration

Create a script for the narration that tells the story, using the sound bites as you would use quotes in an article, or simply script the arrangement of the sound bites. How do you know what your opening sound bite should be? It's pretty simple—the strongest, most compelling one you have. Choose the quote that best tells what the story is about. Once the script is in place, I use the video-editing software's timeline to edit the clips and place them in order. Then I record my narration with a Blue Microphone Snowball mic, which sells for $100 and plugs into the USB port. It sounds much stronger than the mic from the internal webcam (see Chapter 3).

Add the B-roll

Now, the biggest part of the process begins—illustrating the narration. I usually grab still photos, B-roll, and online videos to appear on screen with my voiceover.

For example, in late 2011 in San Francisco, I went to do a piece on the red-hot photo-sharing app Instagram. It was the day after Apple unveiled its new iPhone 4S, with its new and improved camera, so Instagram was poised to gain even more followers.

The interview was with Instagram founder Kevin Systrom, who talked about his humble beginnings (before he sold the firm to Facebook for $1 billion), and demonstrated how to use the app.

When I got back to my computer, I used the narration as an introduction, a way to let viewers know what they were about to see. My script: "Instagram, which turns your iPhone photos from ho-hum to ultra-cool, is the most popular photo app for the iPhone, with over 10 million downloads. And that was before the release of the iPhone 4S. If any app maker has reason to cheer the new iPhone, it's Instagram."

Figure 8.6 In videos about apps and other software, showing features in action makes for good B-roll footage.

To illustrate, I used B-roll of photos on the iPhone that were being "Instagrammed" (*Figure 8.6*) with fun filters along with screen captures of Instragram's No. 1 ranking in the iTunes App Store and the Apple website touting the iPhone 4S. (I captured the screen with SnapzPro software.) Then, I cut to the first sound bite from Systrom.

In the video, I used three sound bites from Systrom from our sit-down interview along with bites from two extended segments. First, we got video of me shooting pictures of Systrom on an iPhone as he used the Instagram app. Then, he and I sat together and walked through the process of jazzing up the photo with Instagram filters. The process took one or two minutes, but I only wanted to show 10 or 15 seconds on the video.

So, I cut to the main points and used graphics, just as I'm doing in this book. To show the process in the video, I inserted graphics (*Figure 8.7*):

- Step 1: Select the Picture.
- Step 2: Choose a Filter.
- Step 3: Save and Share.

Figure 8.7 During the interview, the app's cofounder and I looked at the app together.

USING SIMPLE VIDEO-EDITING SOFTWARE

Now, I will give you a quick overview of the popular, free video programs, Movie Maker and iMovie. Then, I will review a more full-featured yet inexpensive alternative, Adobe Premiere Elements.

Using clips supplied at www.peachpit.com/videonation you can perform some basic trims in iMovie or Elements plus add cutaway shots and titles. In the next chapter, we'll get even more advanced with Apple's Final Cut Pro X, the software I use every day to produce the "Talking Tech" videos for *USA TODAY*.

Movie Maker for Windows

I feel obliged to mention this software because it's free—and it could be useful if you don't own a video-editing program and you want to learn the basics of editing. Movie Maker, available as a free download from Microsoft, is so bare bones that you can do little beyond making a simple trim in a clip, adding titles and silly effects, and then exporting the video to the web (*Figure 8.8*). Once you're finished with the project, you can only save the file in Windows Media Video format, which is lower resolution and quality than other formats.

NOTE My mother loves Movie Maker, as you'll see in the section "Meet the Bloggin', Vloggin' Grandma," at the end of this chapter.

Figure 8.8 Movie Maker is a popular, free program for getting your feet wet and doing a very basic edit on a project. Microsoft plans to support Movie Maker for Windows 8.

Since we have grander ambitions, let's pass on this one. If you have Windows, please try Adobe Premiere Elements instead, which retails for $99 and is often available at a discounted price. Other low-budget choices include Pinnacle Studio HD ($60) and Sony Vegas Studio HD ($50).

iMovie for Mac

Apple iMovie was reconfigured in 2007 after an Apple engineer went on vacation and returned with a brainstorm. He realized that people rarely edited videos for a good reason— because it was too hard. So he started redesigning the interface, creating one that lets you view all the frames of your shots by just skimming the cursor over the footage. So now, you can decide which portions of video to use by dragging the mouse over the section. The updated iMovie interface features a new take on the traditional timeline that video editors have used for years.

The iMovie program comes free with new Macs and is thought to be in use on more than 50 million computers. Look for the Star icon on the Mac dock to launch it. (A light, bare-bones version of iMovie is also available for the iPhone, iPad, and iPod Touch, which you'll learn about later in this chapter..)

NOTE If you want to follow along in the next section using real footage, download the Chapter08 files from www.peachpit.com/videonation.

Step-by-step editing in iMovie

In the iMovie window, the raw video displays at the bottom in the Event browser and the edited video displays at the top in the Project browser (*Figure 8.9*). Buttons for adding music, photos, titles, and transitions to the project are provided below the Viewer. Here are the basic steps for creating an Event and editing your footage:

Watch the video available at www.peachpit.com/videonation to learn how to edit your footage in iMovie.

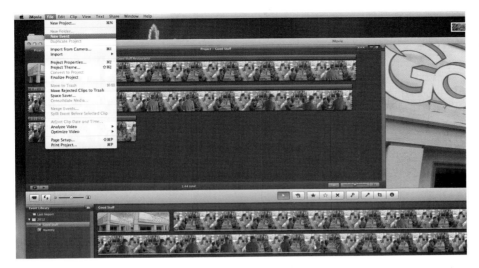

Figure 8.9 The raw
video files appear
in the bottom of the
interface in what's
called the Event
browser.

Figure 8.10 Name
your event in the
Event Library, which
is at the lower left in
the interface.

1   First, create an event (File > New Event) and name it in the Event Library.
    Because the event for this example is a meeting with Good Stuff restaurants
    owner, Cris Bennett, call the event "Good Stuff" (Figure 8.10).

2   Now, you'll import the files for this project from the Cris Interview folder on
    your drive (you can download these files from www.peachpit.com/videona-
    tion). In iMovie, choose File > Import > Movies and locate the three Good Stuff
    files to import (GS_1.mov, GS_2.mov, and GS_3.mov). Be sure to add the movies
    to the Good Stuff event and then click Import.

Figure 8.11 Create your project and then select a theme (or don't select a theme at all).

3 Create a project (File > New Project) and call it Good Stuff.

While working in the project, you take your raw video files and edit them into the final—you guessed it—project. This is where you make your trims, adjust color and lighting, add titles, and so on. When selecting a project, iMovie will offer you a bunch of choices. You can choose different "themes" for the video that will result in specific graphical bumpers that show up when you select titles (*Figure 8.11*). (For example, Comic Book is bright and garish, Newscast looks like the local news, and Photo Album is scrapbooky.) When you choose a theme, iMovie automatically adds titles and backgrounds for each specific theme. I usually choose No Theme, so I can make the various title and graphics choices as I go along.

4 Your entire shoot, with the clips imported, is in the Event browser at the bottom of the iMovie window. To find the good parts, you can play the clips by hitting the spacebar.

TIP You can watch the entire clip in fast-forward by simply dragging the cursor across the clip.

5 Pick a section you like by using the mouse to highlight it (in yellow), and drag it to the Project area (*Figure 8.12*). Let's do this together, with the GS_1.mov file. This clip features the outdoor Good Stuff sign, which I shot on a Canon point-and-shoot, while on roller blades. The beginning is very shaky, but it smooths out, at approximately 4 seconds in. Select the clip after the first 4 seconds and drag it to the Project browser.

6 Now we're ready for our next clip. Insert GS_2 directly after GS_1. It's a wide shot of the restaurant and kids being served food.

Figure 8.12
You can select the exact portion of the clip you want to use by dragging the yellow handles on the clip with your mouse and placing the clip in the Project Library.

Figure 8.13 Creating a cutaway is simple if you follow just a few steps.

7 Let's add a quick, basic cutaway shot. Important—you won't be able to add a cutaway before doing this first: Choose Preferences from the iMovie menu. In the General tab, check Show Advanced Tools, so you can add cutaways, picture in picture, chapter markers, and even green screen. Doing this allows you to add these goodies later.

8 Our cutaway shot is GS_3, another angle of the kids at the booth. Before we add it, the first thing we want to do is delete the audio, so it doesn't compete with GS_2. With the GS 3 clip selected, choose Clip > Mute Clip to kill the audio.

9 Now, drag GS_3 directly on top of GS_2. When the context menu pops up, choose Cutaway (*Figure 8.13*). Now you've inserted your B-roll. Drag the shot to the exact position you want it—I'd like GS_3 to be directly over the beginning of GS_2.

And that's a basic edit. Normally, we would continue with several other scenes, but we have much more material to dive into, so let's call it a day here and add a title and transition.

Pretty it up

Now, you will add a title to the beginning of the project.

1   Click the Title Browser button in the iMovie Project browser (*Figure 8.14*).

2   You'll see many choices. Choose Lower Third (*Figure 8.15*).

Figure 8.14 Add a title by first clicking the Title Browser button.

Figure 8.15 Choose a title such as Lower Third for a professional look.

3 Drag the title directly onto the clip in your Timeline.

4 Depending on where you drag the title, you will see a blue highlight on the clip that shows where the title is added—at the beginning, over the entire clip, or at the end (*Figure 8.16*).

5 Select the blue highlighted title in the Timeline by clicking it.

6 Go to the Viewer to type in the text. In this case, simply type "Good Stuff" on the first line, and "Restaurants" on the second line. This is what's called a lower third credit, because it takes up the lower third of the screen (*Figure 8.17*).

Figure 8.16 The blue highlight shows where you can edit your text.

Figure 8.17 The lower third for the Good Stuff project.

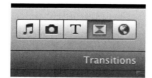

Figure 8.18 Add a transition by clicking the Transition button.

Now, you will put a transition between the GS_1 and GS_2 clips in the Project.

1 Click the Transition button (*Figure 8.18*).
2 Select the first choice, the Cross Dissolve.
3 Drag the transition onto the Timeline, between the two clips.
4 Complete the project with a fade-out transition. From the transitions list, simply select and drag Fade to Black to the end of the clip, and you'll get a great, professional-looking fade-out.

Share it

Once you're satisfied with your edited video, you can choose the Share tab from the File menu to do a one-click upload to YouTube. Or you can choose from other options, such as saving a full-resolution QuickTime version to your specifications. I usually pick the 1280x720 aspect ratio, which is one step down from full HD that gives you a great-looking web video in a reasonable-size file—usually around 100 MB or so. (With this choice, you can also play the video on the iPhone 4S, the second- and third-generation iPad, and the fourth-generation iPod Touch.)

LIMITATIONS OF iMOVIE

While it's a great program, there are a few things you should be aware of that you *can't* do with iMovie:

- Have multiple video tracks. You can use an insert shot as demonstrated for a cutaway, but you can't also add your company logo as a watermark, or another piece of video across the screen and another underneath. The B-roll cutaway technique demonstrated works, but you'll have finer control over your B-roll in other video programs.

- Make a DVD of your final project directly from iMovie. Apple has discontinued the iDVD software, so to make a DVD you'll have to look to third-party choices such as Roxio's Toast software.

Figure 8.19 Adobe Premiere Elements offers access to multiple video and audio tracks, as well as greater control of cutaway shots.

Adobe Premiere Elements

Adobe Premiere Elements, which retails for $99, is my favorite all-around choice for the budget videomaker who wants to go beyond iMovie, but doesn't have the scratch to spring for Final Cut Pro X. Elements is available for both Windows and Mac (*Figure 8.19*).

All the things I just mentioned that you can't do in iMovie—such as greater control of the B-roll cutaway shots, use of multiple video tracks, and burning a DVD of your final project—you can easily do in Elements.

What I don't like about Elements is this: In targeting consumers, Adobe made Elements too "silly" for my tastes. When I'm reaching for a title, for example, I want just plain text. Elements, however, puts words in clouds and bubbles, taking away any professional sheen to the lettering.

In addition, Elements opens lots of tabs when you start the program, urging you to employ a useless organizer that gets in the way of starting your project. The software tries so hard to be consumer friendly that I feel like it makes things harder, not easier. Adobe offers so many choices when importing files—DV camcorder, Flipcam, Webcam, Digital Still Camera, and more—that your eyes get exhausted before you finally get to, duh, File.

Still, for the purposes of what we're discussing here, you can do pretty much everything you want in Elements. To get around the silly lettering and pre-interface welcome, you can always create your own lettering in Adobe Photoshop or another program, and import it as a separate JPG file.

Let's take a closer look.

Watch the video available at www.peachpit. com/videonation to learn more about editing in Premiere Elements.

Getting started in Premiere Elements

Premiere Elements is a classic, timeline-based video editor. Your clips go on a big board, which stretches across the screen. The audio track displays under the video. You can build upon both by adding multiple tracks for cutaways, watermarks, titles, and more.

As in iMovie, you create a new project, name it, and then import your footage. (You'll import footage in the step-by-step section that comes next.) Once your footage is imported, you'll see your clips in the Project window.

The main window offers two choices, Sceneline and Timeline. Choose the traditional Timeline option. You'll see a group of lines, Video 1, Video 2, Audio 1, and so on. These are the multiple sources of video and audio we just discussed (*Figure 8.20*).

Directly under the video monitor and to the right, there are three tools; the first two will be important to you (*Figure 8.21*):

- Use the Split Clip tool (which looks like a scissors) to trim and split the clip.

- Use the Title tool to type text over the video.

- Use the Freeze Frame tool to make an instant still photo from a frame.

Figure 8.20 The traditional Timeline view allows you to see all your video and audio tracks.

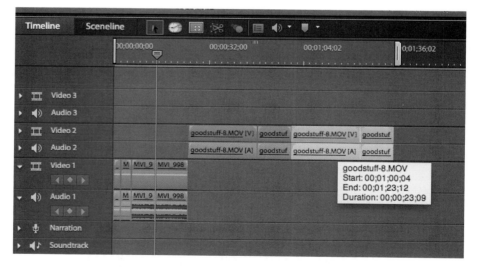

Figure 8.21 Split clips using the Split Clip tool.

While you may not use them as often, there are other useful tools that are not in the Project section, but rather in the Edit section. There you'll find buttons for Effects (auto color, black and white, old film), transitions (dissolves, cube spins, and the like), and themes, including generic templates like the ones in iMovie.

Step-by-step editing in Premiere Elements

So now let's go back to the Project tab and start editing our video clips of the Good Stuff shoot.

1 Import the three supplied clips from the Peachpit website (GS_1, GS_2, and GS_3) by choosing File > Get Media From > Files and Folders. Navigate to the three files and click Import.

2 Drag GS_1 to the Timeline to the Video 1 and Audio 1 track.

3 Play GS_1 by selecting it and tapping the spacebar.

4 Now, let's delete the first four seconds of GS_1 to get rid of the shaky footage. You'll use the Split Clip tool (refer to Figure 8.21) to split the first part of the clip that leads up to that moment. Do this by lining up the playhead over your desired edit point, and clicking the Split Clip tool. Then delete the portion you're not using (the first 4 seconds) by highlighting the section and pressing the Delete key.

5 Drag GS_3 to the timeline, right next to GS_1.

6 Now let's add our cutaway shot like we did with iMovie. In this case, we just place the GS_2 clip directly atop GS_3, on the next level up (*Figure 8.22*).

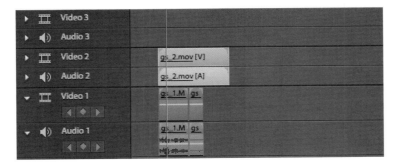

Figure 8.22 Add a cutaway shot and place the GS_2 clip directly above the GS_3 clip.

Figure 8.23
Use the Selection tool to drag the text to the lower-left corner of your video.

7 Right-click (Windows) or Control-click (Mac) the new clip, and select Delete Audio.

8 Click the Text tool in the Monitor.

9 Choose a font (good luck!) and type "Good Stuff Restaurants." You can also choose a font size or change the spacing between characters.

10 Select the Selection tool (the arrow pointing upward) and drag the text down to the lower-left corner of the video. This will give you a lower thirds title (*Figure 8.23*).

11 You're not really done—but for this section you are. So let's save and export this little clip for the web. From the Share tab on the top right of the screen, choose from basic web uploads to sites such as YouTube or Facebook, or you can pick the specific file format of your choice and save to your computer. For more on uploading to the web, see Chapter 10.

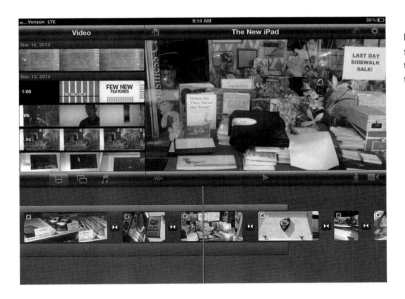

Figure 8.24 The iPad version of iMovie allows you to make basic cuts and add titles, effects, and transitions.

EDITING VIDEO ON THE IPHONE, IPAD, AND IPOD TOUCH

Apple sells a $4.99 version of iMovie for the iPhone, iPad, and iPod Touch that lets you make really simple edits on the fly. For the price of a coffee drink, it's a steal (*Figure 8.24*). The app isn't as full featured as the computer version, but you can still make basic cuts, add titles and effects, and get a fully finished video within minutes. You also get a choice of several minimal templates—with supplied music backgrounds—to dress up your videos.

Using templates is a good news, bad news thing. While they can seem helpful, so few templates are available, and so many people have used them, that using them makes you look like a plagiarizer. I'd skip them.

Step-by-Step Editing with the iMovie App

Let's take a look at the steps involved with editing on the iPad. First, let's assume you've shot some video footage with your iPhone, iPad, or iPod Touch. The files reside in the Camera Roll section of the device. You can also import them onto your computer by synchronizing your device with iTunes.

1 On the iMovie Home screen, tap the plus (+) sign and choose New Project.

2 Tap the Filmstrip icon to add media.

3 Select a clip you want to use and tap the blue arrow to add media to the browser.

Learn about editing using iMovie on the iPad by watching the video at www.peachpit.com/videonation.

4   You can continue to add clips by selecting the Filmstrip icon at the top of the screen. Theme, select Project Settings. Your choices are Modern, Bright, etc.

5   To add a Theme, select Project Settings by tapping the gear icon on the top right of the screen. Your choices are Modern, Bright, etc.

6   Trimming takes some getting used to. In the timeline, you double tap the clip and yellow handles appear around the clip. You can move the handles with your fingers to trim the left and right sides of the clip.

7   To add a title to the video, tap the beginning of the clip. The Clip Settings dialog box will display specify whether you want the title to run at the opening, middle, or end of the clip (*Figure* 8.25). You can even pick a location for your clip.

8   Add a transition next. There aren't many choices here. But in the same dialog box as for the themes, if you select Fade In From Black and Fade Out To Black, you'll get an open and closing transition.

9   When you're ready to share your video with the world, click the Star button at the top left of the screen and it will take you back to the main iMovie splash screen. Here, look for your new project, which probably has no name.

You have a choice of going directly to sites such as YouTube and Facebook, or sending it to the device's Camera Roll by tapping the right-facing arrow at the bottom of the screen. Somewhere along the line, the YouTube and Facebook uploads tend to get screwed up in the transfer. I prefer having the control to export it as a full-resolution video. Then, I pull it out of the Camera Roll when I've connected the device to the computer.

Figure 8.25 Add a title to your edited video on the iPad.

REAL-WORLD SCENARIO:
THE BLOGGIN', VLOGGIN' GRANDMA

I'd like to introduce you to someone who has ignored every bit of videomaking advice I've given—yet is laughing all the way to the bank. Meet my mother, Judy Graham, in her 75th year as I'm writing this book. Judy is known to legions of YouTube fans for "KnittingtipsbyJudy," her weekly lessons on how to make things with yarn and needles (*Figure 8.26*).

Figure 8.26
Knitting Tips by Judy is a practical video tutorial series.

So far, Judy has pulled in more than 6 million views for her extremely low-tech videos. External microphone? Wouldn't dream of it. Tripod? Why bother? B-roll and cutaway shots? Whatchyou talkin' about?

Best of all, Google adds advertising to her videos and gives her 51 percent of the revenues, earning her thousands of dollars a year—enough to pay her annual real estate taxes. Not bad for a hobby.

How It Started

My mom started making videos at my suggestion. I had just written an article for *USA TODAY* about seniors making money by creating websites that feature ads from Google. It's part of the search giant's AdSense network that Google created to raise its advertising to greater heights. Companies agree to put Google ads on their websites in return for a cut of the dollars. In turn, Google grows its empire. Judy Graham was intrigued and wanted to try something that could bring in money, too.

Watch an interview with the "Knitter to the Stars," Judy Graham, in the video at www.peachpit.com/videonation.

After my parents divorced in the 1970s, my mom started a second act as a knitter. She moved to Los Angeles and started making sweaters, scarves, and hats for Hollywood productions such as the TV series "Rhoda" and, most notably, the movie *Nightmare on Elm Street*. She made that red-and-black striped sweater that Freddy Krueger is known for (*Figure 8.27*).

After reading my article, my mom was inspired. We talked about what she could do, and it just seemed so obvious. Since she knew knitting so well, why not create a website about knitting, offering lessons for people who wanted to know how to make sweaters, scarves, and the like? So she and her life partner, Mike Ansell, went to work making it. Lots of competition exists in knitting lessons—in text form. So when Judy and Mike decided to start making videos, they found their niche.

Figure 8.27 My mom's creation—the Freddy Krueger sweater.

Figure 8.28 The website started out very simple and basic.

Figure 8.29 Obviously, it's important to show close-up detail such as this in a knitting video.

Production Values

Judy and Mike's initial videos were shaky and so basic that you could hear Mike whispering the cue "OK" to my mom at the beginning of the shoot (*Figure 8.28* and *Figure 8.29*). But viewers didn't care. They hungered for the knitting knowledge she had to offer. They also didn't need to know about her Hollywood background, even though Mike liberally sprinkled words such as "Knitter to the Stars" on the website to try for better Google rankings. What viewers really wanted to know was how to make lace and bamboo stitches.

Gear

Over the years, Judy and Mike upgraded from a $99 Canon point-and-shoot that captured video in standard definition to a $160 Panasonic Lumix that captures HD video (*Figure 8.30*).

They make the videos in their very quiet Hollywood home, with no external sound sources to compete with, so they don't even use an external microphone. "If we were outside," says Mike, "then sure, we'd use a mic. The sound would be terrible."

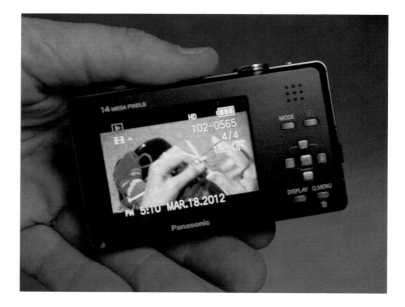

Figure 8.30 You don't need an expensive camera to get good shots.

The Shoot

Download the video at www.peachpit.com/videonation to see how the author set up his interview of Judy.

On shoot days, my mom sits in a white rocking chair. She wears a black skirt because the yarn and stitches show up better over a solid, dark color (*Figure 8.31*). Her hands clutch two needles and some yarn as Mike stands over her with the camera, looking down at her hands (*Figure 8.32*). She narrates and demonstrates as he records.

All in all, Judy and Mike spend about three minutes on the videos, only stopping if an airplane soars overhead or another noisy distraction occurs.

As noted earlier, they left me out of the production process and developed the shoots and segments all on their own. Had I been there, I would have urged a three-camera shoot, fancy titles, and graphics. But they want to be as low-tech as possible.

Mike lights the scene with a Smith-Victor A100 continuous-light lamp ($82.95 at B&H) with a $7.95 Ushio EBW 500-watt daylight-balanced lightbulb.

"We are a perfect example of how basic it can be," Mike says.

Mike edits the videos, slicing out his instructions and any flubs, and inserting an open and close. He started off editing in Windows Movie Maker, but found it too limiting. He switched to Adobe Premiere Elements, and now he uses iMovie.

Mike does know his way around the camera. His day job is as a set photographer for TV shows, using professional cameras from Canon, such as the 7D. For these videos at home, however, he believes simple works best. "I love that the Panasonic is a true point-and-shoot," he says. "It couldn't be any easier. It works perfectly for what we need to do."

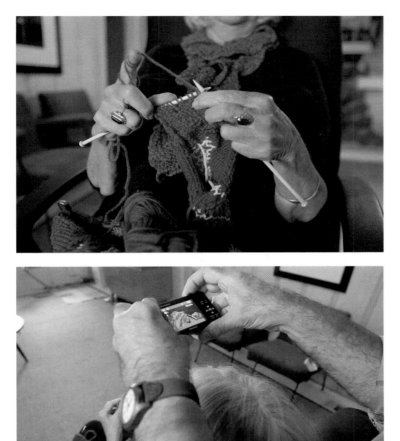

Figure 8.31 Good contrast makes for a more interesting video.

Figure 8.32 Recall the importance of good camera placement.

The Editing Process

After Mike is done shooting, he edits the video in iMovie during a very simple, quick once-over. He takes out his audio cues and any bumps along the way—like flubbed words that were re-recorded.

He doesn't use transitions or graphics to show the different steps she's talking about in the video. He wants to keep the process as simple as possible. In fact, he switched from Adobe Premiere Elements to iMovie because the titling process was speedier, he says.

In iMovie, when he's done with trimming—which takes about 15 minutes— Mike chooses an orange background from the Theme section. In the title area, he opts for Centered, the first choice. He clicks Share to save the video as a full 1080p HD video to his desktop, and copies it to a flash drive.

Mike hands the flash drive to my mom, so she can start uploading and promoting it. She used to try posting the videos everywhere—YouTube plus other video sites such as Vimeo and Howcast—but the action was clearly at YouTube, so she puts all her energies there.

Judy uploads the videos to the Howto & Style section of YouTube, fills in the descriptions with keywords, using phrases such as *knitting, knitting videos, knittingtipsbyjudy, topaz knitwear* (the name of her company), and *Judy Graham*. This lets YouTube know what the videos are about, makes them more searchable, and identifies the type of ads that should appear in them. Surprisingly, their videos attract the biggest, mainstream advertisers, such as Wells Fargo Bank, Honda, Nautica, and Jaguar.

Promotion

After uploading the video, Judy gets to work sending out updates to her YouTube and Facebook subscribers. Once people know the new video is out, she starts planning the next one.

I asked her if ideas come from her fans—surely, they have suggestions.

They do, she said, but she has so many ideas about knitting, she's not hurting for material. And since the newer videos in HD look so much better than the earlier ones, they're looking at redoing the first batch in HD. As with many folks with large YouTube audiences, her first video (on the casting on technique) is the most viewed. To date, it's had 400,000 views.

According to Judy, it took about six months for the videos to start getting discovered on YouTube. They just kept on making them, and plugging them anywhere online they could, hoping for word of mouth. The idea was that if she kept posting notes about it on Facebook and YouTube, friends would tell others and traffic would eventually build.

And that's what happened. At first, Google started paying her pennies and single dollars each week. By the next year, they were up to hundreds, and now they're looking at thousands each year.

Dealing with Google, however, is like trying to communicate with the Wizard of Oz. You work hard and do your best, but you don't know why, for instance, you might get a bigger check for your Tuesday videos than for your Thursday videos. Google doesn't spell out how a video makes the ad cut. There's nobody to call for advice. The communication is all via email, and often the responses come from a help desk outside the country.

Regardless of ads and responses, viewers have been pouring on the praise. "Thank you so much," wrote Laurie Wilkinson on the YouTube KnittingtipsbyJudy page. "You are a life-saver. Your tips, videos, and instruction are invaluable. I find I go to them again and again."

"Thanks a big bunch Judy for showing us how to do this stitch," wrote craftymom7.

The Latest

Now, with one successful channel under her belt, Judy's onto a second channel—a vlog (video blog).

"My son said, 'What's the matter with you, you only have one channel?'" she recalls being told, over lunch in Hermosa Beach at the fabulous Good Stuff Restaurant. "You've got to do more."

I did, indeed, suggest that if iJustine and the Annoying Orange have second channels, why shouldn't KnittingtipsbyJudy? After all, if YouTube exposure was paying for her real estate taxes, why not try to up it and pay for lunch and desserts, too?

"Just talk about what you're working on," I said. "Surely if you have these hundreds of thousands of people watching your lessons, they might be interested in seeing your face and hearing you talk about whatever's going on in your life."

So she started vlogging.

The Vlog Process

"I do it twice a week," Judy says. "And I do just talk about whatever's going on in my world of knitting. It's been really fun. I talk into the webcam on my PC, and edit the video afterwards. I insert an open and close, and I'm so proud of myself."

On the vlog, instead of showing a project in motion, she talks about what she plans to make, such as new scarves and blankets that are in the works.

The vlog doesn't get the same kind of views—her most successful garnered 900 viewers—"but people seem to be interested, and I get great feedback."

Judy records her thoughts directly into Movie Maker, which connects to her webcam on a cheap Dell laptop. With the video directly on the timeline, she chooses an open and close from the Theme menu, and adds a title for the beginning and end. Then, she chooses the one-click upload to YouTube and sends it up to the cloud.

Just think about how Google and YouTube have changed the world. My mom could be sitting around the house, playing canasta, and watching "The View" and other talk shows on TV. Instead, with a cheap laptop, the most basic software, and an Internet connection, she's created her own channel, from her very own home.

And how cool is that?

ADVANCED VIDEO EDITING

9

IN THE PREVIOUS CHAPTER, we looked at how to do basic Timeline edits. We trimmed clips and added transitions, titles, and B-roll cutaway shots in Apple iMovie and Adobe Premiere Elements.

Now, we'll get serious and have some fun by graduating to Final Cut Pro X, the Apple software I use every day to make my "Talking Tech" videos for *USA TODAY*. (Note that Final Cut Pro X is only available for Mac.)

I love Final Cut Pro X for what I like to do—make short videos. It takes way less time to make them using Final Cut Pro X than it did with version 7, the supplied graphics look great, and, most importantly, no software is easier to use for editing multicamera footage.

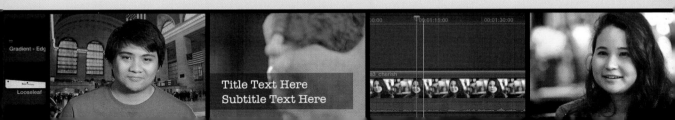

Since I want you all to eventually start producing two-camera and three-camera shoots, the way they do for TV, this chapter covers how to edit those using Final Cut Pro. To try the features first hand, use the clips supplied at www.peachpit.com/videonation.

Note that you don't have to shell out $299 to try Final Cut Pro X—a fully functioning, free 30-day trial version is available at apple.com/finalcutpro. You can skip this chapter if you are not interested in installing or using Final Cut Pro X.

INTRODUCING FINAL CUT PRO X

In a controversial move, Apple overhauled its beloved professional application, Final Cut Pro 7, in June 2011. The software was transformed from a treasured tool for production houses and serious editors into a program also aimed at the much larger consumer audience. As a result, the software is now easier and zippier to use. With tabs to tap into your iTunes and iPhoto libraries, it is clearly designed to speak to the throngs of Apple fans who own iMacs and MacBook Pros. Today, it is a tool consumers can graduate to from iMovie. And that's fine. Most folks won't mind if Final Cut Pro X looks like iMovie as long as it gets the job done. I must admit, I was thrown off at first, but then I started using it.

A Quicker Way to Edit

Final Cut Pro 7 did the job, but was really tough to use because of the dreaded R button—Render! To do something as simple as adding a transition, you had to press Command-R to render it and wait to see the result. In other words, the program would come to a standstill as it processed your changes.

Even moving a clip slightly to the left or right might require a complete render that could take as long as 30 minutes to run—and you couldn't continue to work on your project while this was happening.

In Final Cut Pro X, rendering works in the background—and this is the number one reason I'm such a big fan. Final Cut Pro is still doing its thing, but you get to keep editing. You can see the red render-progress bars at the top of the screen, but the process doesn't generally slow you down, especially if you have a fast computer (*Figure 9.1*).

Figure 9.1 The dreaded red Render process in the old Final Cut Pro 7.

In overhauling Final Cut Pro, Apple evolved the software to suit the workflows of today's video cameras rather than the tape-based cameras of the past. These days, most video workflows involve flash memory rather than tape, whether that be on memory cards from point-and-shoot cameras, DSLRs, most new video cameras, or even Apple devices such as the iPhone, iPad, and iPod Touch.

The Layout

When you launch Final Cut Pro X, you'll see the Event Library on the left and the Viewer on the right (*Figure 9.2*). The Event Library is where you choose clips to use in editing; the Viewer is where you get to see them in action, after an edit. You can play through (Apple calls it "skimming") clips quickly in the Event Library by placing the mouse directly over the thumbnail. Here, you can drag the mouse over the section of your choice and select just that portion for the edit.

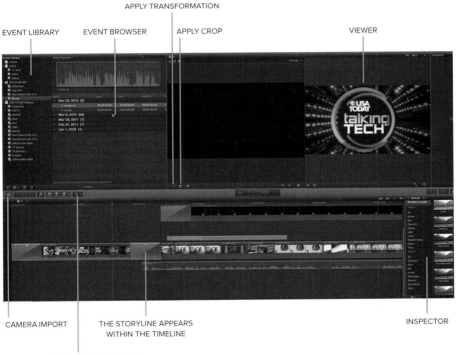

APPLY TRANSFORMATION

EVENT LIBRARY   EVENT BROWSER   APPLY CROP   VIEWER

CAMERA IMPORT   THE STORYLINE APPEARS   INSPECTOR
            WITHIN THE TIMELINE

OTHER USEFUL TOOLS SUCH AS
THE BLADE TOOL ARE LOCATED HERE

Figure 9.2
The Final Cut Pro X interface.

The Final Cut Pro X toolbar provides shortcuts to features such as importing footage, adding transitions, and making basic trims. Here, I will focus on the ones you'll use the most. This is how the icons display onscreen, from left to right (Figure 9.2):

- **Import from Camera:** Click this button if you have connected a camera, such as an iPhone or iPad, an older tape-based camcorder, or a video camera that records in the AVCHD format. Use Camera Import if you want to turn on the webcam and record directly into Final Cut Pro. For cameras that record directly to memory cards, you will import the footage via the File > Import command (covered in a later section).
- **Arrow:** Click the Arrow to access the most common editing tools—including the Blade tool for basic edits (Command-B) and the Position tool (Command-P) for turning off the Magnetic Timeline and moving things around at will.

Just under the Viewer is a set of compositing controls (Figure 9.2). Here, you can adjust the position, scale, and rotation of your clips. You can also reframe your images with the cropping effects.

- **Apply Tranformation:** Click the Apply Transformation button to grab the video and enlarge the image. This comes in handy if you import a photo that only takes up two-thirds of the screen; with Apply Transformation on, you can blow up the photo to full screen.
- **Apply Crop:** Click the Apply Crop button to trim or crop the image or access the cool Ken Burns Effect tool to zoom in and out of a still photo or video clip.

More useful buttons (*Figure 9.3*) can be found to the right of the Viewer (in what's called the Inspector Window). Here, you can modify clips to your heart's content.

- **Auto Enhancements menu:** Fine tunes the color balance and exposure. You can also fix audio issues here.
- **Timing menu:** Slow or speed up your footage.
- **Transitions button:** Add dissolves, wipes, and other effects between clips.
- **Show Titles Browser button:** Add text.
- **Inspector:** Adjust video and audio settings. This includes everything from changing your audio levels to tweaking the scale and size of a video clip.

TIP Point at each button to display its name, otherwise known as a tool tip.

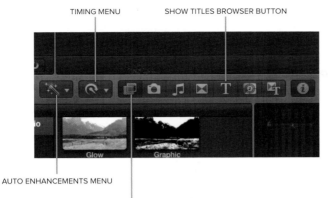

TIMING MENU   SHOW TITLES BROWSER BUTTON

AUTO ENHANCEMENTS MENU

TRANSITIONS BUTTON

Figure 9.3 Even more features can be found to the right of the Viewer.

HANDS ON IN FINAL CUT PRO

This section assumes that you know how to use your camera and connect it to the computer. Here, I'll show you how to put together a simple project in Final Cut Pro X. If you want to follow along, download the clips available at www.peachpit.com/videonation. Once we complete a basic edit, I'll show you how to work with footage from more than one camera—called multicamera editing—because many of you are using a combination of DSLRs, iPhones, point-and-shoot cameras, and video cameras for creating your online projects.

1. Create a Desktop Folder

First, download and unzip the Chapter09 folder from the Peachpit site. Move the folder to your desktop or in the Movies folder. For most projects, you'll want to give this a name that's memorable and tied to your project. Let's name this folder "Judy Video Nation."

2. Create an Event

As with iMovie, you begin with a two-step naming process in Final Cut Pro X. First, choose File > New Event to create and name an event (*Figure* 9.4). Your new event folder appears in the Event Library in the far left column with its name field selected. If you're using the sample clips, name the Event "Judy Knit."

Watch the video available at www.peachpit.com/videonation to learn a few basics about editing in Final Cut Pro X.

Figure 9.4 Create a New Event in Final Cut Pro X.

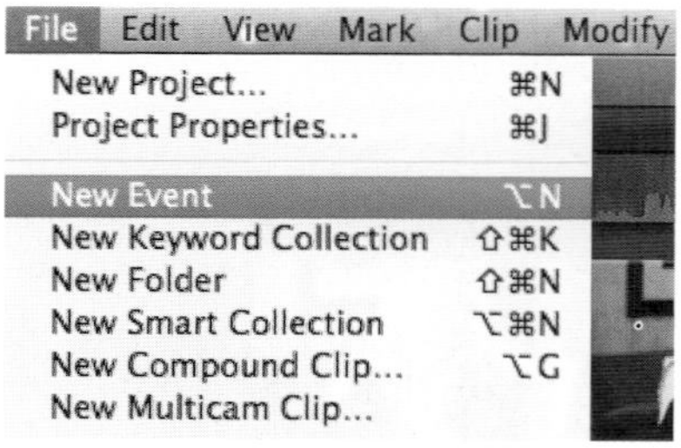

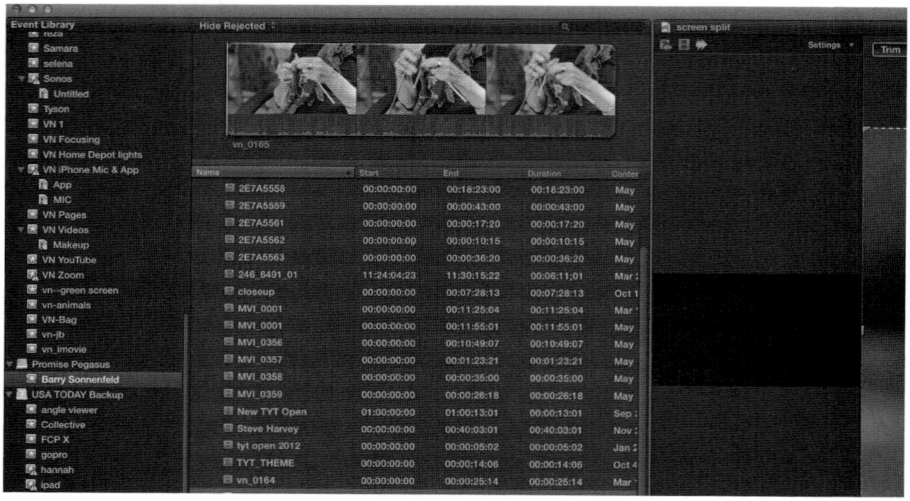

Figure 9.4 shows where your Event Library and Event Browser appear in Final Cut Pro. (You'll import these clips in Step 4.) The Event Library on the left shows all the clips, audio, and graphics you've imported into Final Cut Pro and these are organized into events (basically, an event is a folder containing clips). Everything you add to the Event—your initial clips, plus titles, transitions, and maybe some still photos from iPhoto, end up in this folder, even if they also appear elsewhere on the drive. (So when you're looking to clear room on your drive, after you've finished the projects, look for Final Cut Events. They'll probably be chock-full of gigabytes.)

Figure 9.5 Name your Project in the New Project Window.

3. Create a Project

After you name the event, the next step is to name the Project as well. Choose File > New Project, and name the project "Judy Knit" (*Figure 9.5*). This clears the Timeline for you to start working. The reason for the double naming, according to Apple, is that you might be doing one Project—"Judy DVD," for example—and another, shorter one, "Judy Web," using the same clips.

4. Import Footage

Now, let's import our video clips and screenshot. The import process in Final Cut Pro X is straight and to the point. If you're using the sample clips and following along, simply choose File > Import > Files, navigate to the folder containing the Judy clips, select Judy Knit in the Add to existing event field, and click Import.

If you're working on a different project, here are your import choices:

- **Import Files:** Choose File > Import> Files to select video clips from a hard drive directly into Final Cut Pro or select from an existing iMovie project.

- **Import from Camera:** If you're using an Apple mobile device (such as an iPhone or iMac) or an older connected camera, plug it into the USB or FireWire port of your Mac, and choose File > Import from Camera. Click Import All to bring in all the clips, or just select the ones you want and click Import.

After the import, the clips display in the Event Browser, which is immediately to the right of the Event Library.

A cool enhancement in Final Cut Pro X—first introduced in iMovie, by the way—is that you can hover the cursor over the clip and skim the entire clip. In Final Cut Pro 7, you had to double-click the clip and then click Play. But now, if you're really good with your mouse, you can see the whole thing, in either super fast-forward or normal speed, just by pointing the cursor at the clip. That's one big time-saver.

5. Let's Edit!

During the editing process, you can do many things: create transitions, add a voiceover, include music, adjust the color, insert text and graphics, and more. In this exercise, we're going to select clips, record some audio and add it to the Timeline, trim clips, add a sound bite, include B-roll, add transitions, and include a title.

Record the audio

Let's say you are about to create a video called "Meet the Vlogger." The video will open with narration about my mom, Judy Graham (known as Knittingtipswithjudy on YouTube) over screen captures of her videos and wide shots of her living room. (See the "Bloggin', Vloggin' Grandma" section in Chapter 8 to read more about Judy.)

I always start my projects by writing and recording the narration first. The story takes better shape this way. I would normally urge you to use a real microphone for this, but for the purposes of this exercise, the built-in Mac mic will do if that's all you have.

Choose Window > Record Audio. The Record Audio window opens. Click the Destination menu to select the project you want the new audio file to be saved ("Judy Knit"). Select the Built-in Microphone from the Input Device menu. Click the Ready to record button and say the following words into the computer (*Figure 9.6*):

"At age 75, Judy Graham has found herself a new and thriving career. She makes how-to-knit videos that she posts on YouTube, and they've been viewed more than 6 million times. Best of all, by participating in ad revenues, she is bringing in thousands of dollars yearly."

Stop recording by clicking the Record button again. That's your first narration, which will go at the beginning of the piece. The audio clip will automatically appear on the Timeline once you've finished recording. Exit the Record Audio window by clicking the small x in the left corner of the window.

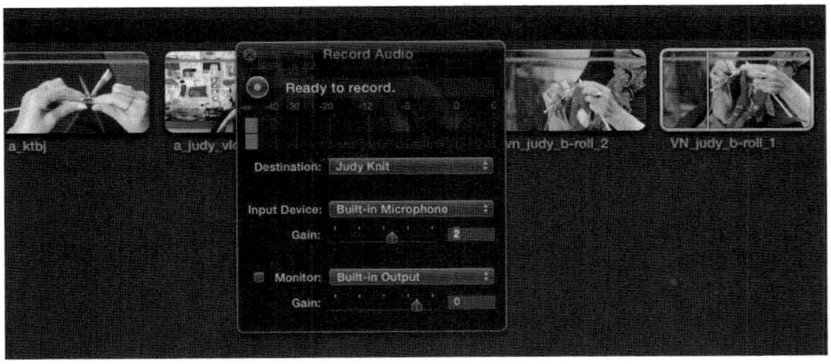

Figure 9.6 Recording an audio track is a simple task in Final Cut Pro X.

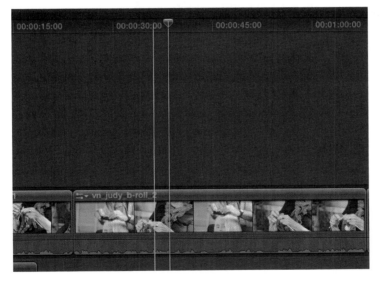

Figure 9.7 Place the clips on the Timeline, just above the audio clip.

Figure 9.8 Move the play-head to the spot where you want to cut the clip.

Illustrate the narration and trim clips

In the Event Browser, choose the three Judy B-roll.mov video clips and drag them onto the Timeline, directly above the audio clip (*Figure 9.7*).

Now, you will cut the portions of the three clips to best tell the story over the audio. You want to cut the clips so they match the length of the audio. To trim these clips, put the playhead (*Figure 9.8*) over where you want the cut to begin and press Command-B (or click the Blade tool). Repeat this process where you want the clip to end. Delete the unused portions of the clip by selecting that portion on the Timeline and pressing the Delete key. Do that for all three clips until you get the "b-roll" coverage you like and the clips match the length of the audio. (You can also choose Edit > Trim Start and Edit > Trim End from the File menu to chop off the beginning or end of a clip in one action.)

Add a sound bite

Select a_closeup.mov from the Event Browser and drag it onto the Timeline after the other clips you just trimmed. At the beginning of the new clip you hear me say, "Meet the vlogger." Advance a few sentences and you'll hear Judy say at approximately 26 seconds into the clip, "I have made over 150 videos in the last two-and-a-half years. I started doing this because my son told me I needed to do this. So I've always been a knitter. I knew how to knit. So I thought, why not teach other people to do as I do? And that's how it got started." This is the sound bite we want on the Timeline.

Make a trimmed clip as you did in the previous section by clicking Command-B just as Judy says "I have made...", and then again after Judy says "started" (approximately 50 seconds in). Now, delete the rest of the clip.

Add more B-roll

You will now put B-roll over the interview clip of Judy. Select a_ktbj in the Event Browser, the close-up of Judy knitting, and drag it directly above a_closeup.mov, one row above. Control-click the clip and choose Detach Audio from the context menu. Now, delete the audio track by selecting the audio that detached and pressing the Delete key. You want the B-roll to be silent. Place the B-roll clip over my mom talking about knitting wherever you like, and make a cut (see the previous section, "Illustrate the narration and trim clips" for how to do this), keeping it to about five to ten seconds (*Figure 9.9*).

Figure 9.9 Place the B-roll above the clips of Judy knitting.

Figure 9.10 Insert a transition between clips.

Add transitions

The simplest transition and the one most used in videos is the cross dissolve. You can easily add a cross dissolve by selecting the clip (which highlights it) and then Right-clicking and choosing Add a Cross Dissolve from the context menu.

Or, you can click the Transitions button under the Viewer, and choose from one of the many transitions, such as Cube, Doorway, Lens Flare, and Flip.

Pick your transition and drag it directly onto the Timeline by inserting it over the ends of the two video clips (*Figure 9.10*). Go ahead and put a cross dissolve at the opening of the video, the first clip, to fade in. Put the same transition at the tail end, for a fadeout.

Add titles

To add titles to your production, click the T button (the Show Titles Browser button) under the Viewer to display a host of title style choices (*Figure 9.11*). In journalism, we like a "lower third" credit (see Chapter 7), which works great for videos posted by bloggers and Facebookers, too. For the title choice, the Information Bar choice is solid and to the point, without looking too cutesy— which several of the Final Cut Pro X title choices are. For my "Talking Tech" shows, I use News-centered, which looks pretty snazzy, flashing in and across the screen.

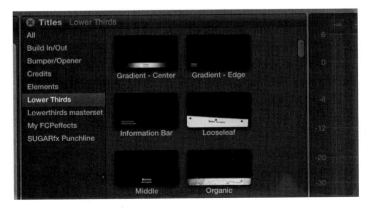

Figure 9.11 For this project, click Lower Thirds to access the Lower Thirds title choices.

To add the title, select one, drag it directly above the clip where you want it to go (*Figure 9.12*), and then double-click it so you can type in your text (*Figure 9.13*).

Add the Information Bar (Lower Third) above the first clip, and title it "Meet the Vlogger" on the first line, and "Judy Graham/Knitting Tips By Judy" on the second line. You have now created a lower third credit (*Figure 9.14*).

Figure 9.12 Drag a title over the clip where you want it to go.

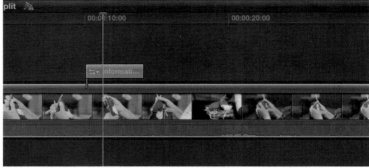

Figure 9.13 Add your lower-third credit to the video clip.

Figure 9.14 The result of adding a title is shown here.

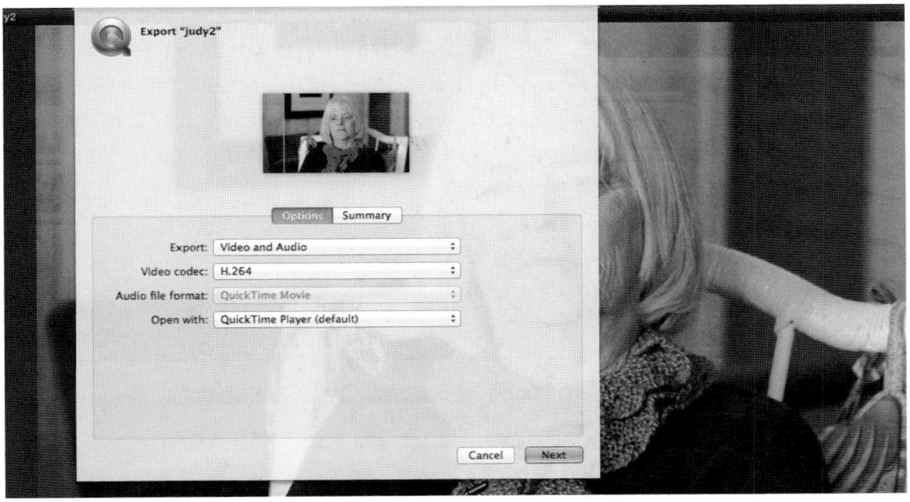

Figure 9.15
The Export options for your completed project.

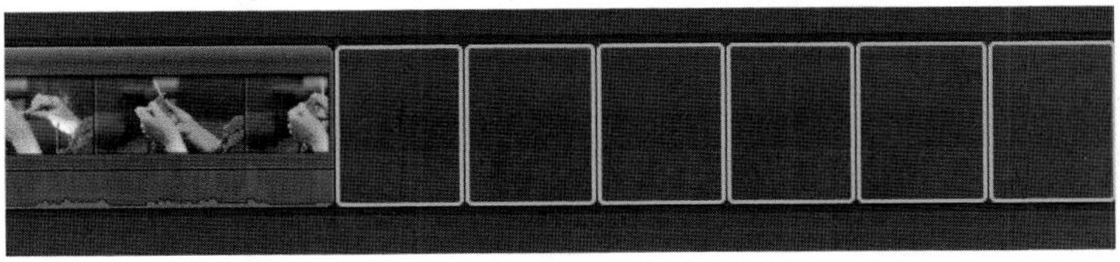

Figure 9.16 Make sure to delete any gaps in your project footage.

6. Share the Video

In reality, we've just gotten started on this clip—it's only about 45 seconds long. Have fun with the supplied clips on the Peachpit website and finish it off. Pull what you think are the three best sound bites and illustrate them with B-roll. Let's see how readers do. I'll have my cut up there as well.

When you've finished the project, it's time to export the video and share it with the world (*Figure 9.15*).

Before you choose Share from the menu bar to export the full, HD-resolution version, here's a quick tip: Look at the last clip and delete anything superfluous on the Timeline, such as extra black gaps that Final Cut Pro X sometimes adds. Not doing this can turn your three-minute video into a nine-minute production—three minutes of video and six minutes of dead air caused by not deleting the gaps (*Figure 9.16*).

In Chapter 10, we'll explore in more detail the process of exporting videos, different file formats, and how to get your projects into video sharing sites such as YouTube and Vimeo.

28:

Watch the video available at www.peachpit.com/videonation to see the author's finished production, Meet the Vlogger.

MULTICAMERA EDITING

At this point, let's take your videos to another level by doing a multicamera edit. Mulitcamera, or multicam, is the shooting technique often seen on TV news-magazines such as "60 Minutes" and "Dateline." The technique usually consists of, at a minimum, a wide shot of the interview, a close-up on the subject, and a medium shot on the reporter.

For this project, my mom was shot in her Los Angeles living room on several cameras—the Canon Rebel EOS T3i, a Canon PowerShot S95, an iPhone, and an iPad. I picked these cameras because they're all consumer devices that most people have access to. I wanted you to see how glorious a multicamera shoot would look, but production issues were a challenge. We set up the four cameras as follows:

- My mom's living room is tight, so I had to figure out how to place four cameras without allowing them be seen in the other shots. We put her in a rocking chair in the middle of the room, lit by afternoon window light, and focused the Rebel EOS T3i, with a 50mm 1.4 lens, directly on her for the close-up. We also had fun shooting her on an iPad, piled high atop a bunch of magazines.
- My shot, a medium, was with the iPhone, which we placed to her side.
- A big wide shot, which is great to cut to, was on the PowerShot S95, which has an amazingly decent wide-angle lens, considering it's a point-and-shoot. This camera was placed by the window, out of the range of the other two cameras.

For sound, we plugged a lav mic into the Rebel, and put my mic into the Zoom audio recorder.

Putting All the Clips Together

To do multicam with Final Cut Pro 7, most savvy editors turned to a great $149 plug-in from Singular Software called Plural Eyes. The tool used the audio cues from the various video tracks to sync them all together. Nine times out of ten, it worked like a charm, and you could then cut accordingly on the Timeline.

Final Cut Pro X, however, offers an even better way to do this, and it's part of the purchase price. You can work like a TV director, choosing between Camera 1, Camera 2, and Camera 3, putting all the multiple angles into your video easily. Here's how to start:

1 Import your clips.

2 Highlight the clips you want.

Figure 9.17 If your productions involve more than one camera, you can use the New Multicam Clip feature in Final Cut Pro X to join up your clips.

3 Choose New Multicam Clip from the File menu.

4 Title it. Wait a few minutes for the clips to be processed and joined together (*Figure 9.17*).

When you choose New Multicam Clip from the File menu, make sure Use Audio for Synchronization is checked. Final Cut Pro puts the different camera angles together by using the audio cues, which usually works pretty well. This does require good, clear sound on all three cameras.

When making a multicamera clip, don't import all your clips into the Event Browser at first. Instead, just choose the ones you want to be joined together at the hip. For the Multicam creation process, you'll highlight what's in the Event Browser. Remember that you can always import the B-roll and secondary footage later.

More on Creating Multicam Clips

You have several options for bringing in the footage and creating the multicam clip. The first and easiest is to select Use Audio for Synchronization when importing the footage. But what if you have a file with poor audio—like if you shot on a PowerShot or an iPhone from far away?

Here's my best advice: Use the marker tool in Final Cut Pro X in the Event Browser to highlight a specific, identical moment in each of the three clips. Look for a section of the clip where, say, you raise your hand. Press the M key to add a marker to that specific spot. Then, find the exact same spot in the other clips and press M again. When that's done, select New Multicam Clip from the File menu, uncheck the Use Audio for Synchronization option, click the Use Custom Settings button, and choose First Marker on the Angle from the Angle Synchronization menu (*Figure 9.18*).

Watch the video available at www.peachpit.com/videonation and learn how to edit multicam clips.

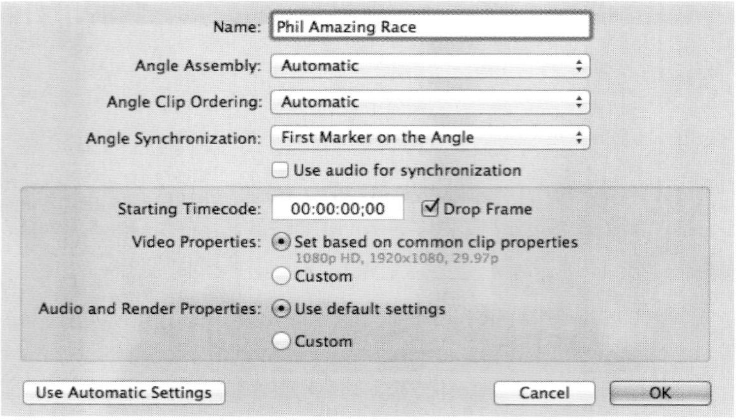

Figure 9.18 You can set a marker to sync the various clips.

Name:	Phil Amazing Race
Angle Assembly:	Automatic
Angle Clip Ordering:	Automatic
Angle Synchronization:	First Marker on the Angle
	☐ Use audio for synchronization
Starting Timecode:	00:00:00;00 ☑ Drop Frame
Video Properties:	⦿ Set based on common clip properties 1080p HD, 1920x1080, 29.97p ◯ Custom
Audio and Render Properties:	⦿ Use default settings ◯ Custom

[Use Automatic Settings]   [Cancel] [OK]

Angle Viewer

With your clips selected and processed, open the Angle Viewer to get a director's view of your production (*Figure 9.19*). The multiple angles are presented in a box, Camera 1, Camera 2, Camera 3, and so on, along with an audio file (if the audio is separate).

Choose Show Angle Viewer from the Window menu, or click Command-Shift-7.

Pick the master clip that you just made—it's whatever you titled it—and put it on the Timeline. You'll see the angles in the Viewer: 1, 2, 3, and 4.

Start playing the clip. To select your angle, press 1 on the keyboard for camera 1, 2 for camera 2, and so on. If you don't like your choice once it's there, press Command-Z to Undo and try again.

Figure 9.19 Use the Angle Viewer to set different views of your production.

Sound Enhancements

You may have different sound on Camera 1 and Camera 2, and need to fix the audio. In the upper-left corner of the Angle Viewer, use the last button, which is a picture of an audio waveform (*Figure 9.20*). This lets you switch between audio. Choose the audio viewer to fine-tune the audio the same way you fine-tune your camera angles.

Play back the clips by pressing the spacebar. At the beginning of each camera switch, click the number that correlates with your track. Fine-tune that way. Once you have the audio issues worked out, you're ready to add titles, B-roll, graphics, and the like, which you've learned how to do by now.

Figure 9.20
Click the third button shown here to work with the audio.

CHROMA KEY EFFECT

Here's one last fun thing to do in Final Cut Pro X: the Chroma Key effect (*Figure 9.21*).

This effect is used when, for example, you want to put yourself in front of the Eiffel Tower or in the middle of Grand Central Station. To do this, you first photograph yourself in front of a green or blue screen, which makes it easy to wipe out the background.

"Screen" is jargon for a backdrop. I have a $99 linen green screen from Backdrop Outlet that I hold up with a backdrop stand. (You can also pin it to the wall.) I also have a $99 blue Chroma Key–like blanket from Westcott, but I prefer the linen because it has fewer creases.

Watch the video available at www.peachpit.com/videonation to discover how to use the Chroma Key effect in Final Cut Pro X.

Figure 9.21
A green screen is helpful for creating productions in which you'll replace the background.

Figure 9.22 Select Keyer to access the Chroma Key features of Final Cut Pro.

Just remember that when doing the Chroma Key effect, you shouldn't wear the color of the backdrop—because the whole point is to eliminate the color of the backdrop (green or blue) in the video.

Also, make sure that the green or blue screen itself is lit. Otherwise, some issues may show up: In one series of videos I made without light on the green screen, moving matter is flying across my jacket, and my hair looked really weird. One simple light aimed at the green screen fixed that.

In Final Cut Pro X, using the Chroma Key effect is fairly easy. Just import the footage with the green or blue background into your Project, click the Effects button (under the Viewer), select Keying, and then select Keyer (*Figure 9.22*).

Double-click the Keyer to make the background black. To try something different in the background—say, the still image of Grand Central Station—find the image, import it, and stick it on the Timeline, directly under the video file you just Chroma Keyed.

Fine-tune the effect by going to the Inspector window (*Figure 9.23*) and adjusting the sliders in the video section until you get it where you like it (*Figure 9.24*).

TIP For more Final Cut Pro X tips, go to http://help.apple.com/finalcutpro/mac/ or read Peachpit's Final Cut Pro X: Making the Transition by Larry Jordan or Final Cut Pro X: Visual QuickStart Guide by Lisa Brenneis and Michael Wohl.

Figure 9.23
Make adjustments to your key in the Inspector.

Figure 9.24
The replaced image achieved using the Chroma Key effect.

SHARING THE
FINAL PRODUCT

10

AT THIS POINT, we've gone over what type of gear to use; how to set up your cameras, lights, and sound when you arrive at the location; and how to prepare questions for an interview. We've also looked at different accessories for your gear and how to edit your footage into a masterpiece.

So, now that your piece is finished, you're ready to save the file and share it with your family and friends on the Internet.

In this chapter, first you'll learn how to encode your video for the web—that is, the file format for your video that offers the best playback—and then how to beat the drum and promote it. My hope is you'll make some money for your videomaking efforts, because after reading about all the gear in this book and drooling over the possibilities, you may need it!

EXPORTING VIDEOS

High-end video-editing software usually uses the term "export" for the process of saving your file for playback. Other software calls it "share." Either way, you will choose a file format for the video when saving it on your hard drive or external drive, or uploading it directly to a website such as YouTube or Vimeo.

Choosing a File Format

Before exporting a video, you need to choose a file format. This is when things can get confusing because video software offers a multitude of file and resolution choices—AVI, Windows Media, QuickTime, 1920-by-1280 resolution, 640-by-480 resolution, and so on. How do you know which one to choose?

In most cases, you're looking for H.264, a video-compression format that generally produces an MP4 or MOV file. (This is also known as MPEG-4.) This has replaced the old AVI (Windows) and QuickTime (Apple) as the default standard for the web. An MP4 file looks great in HD and is small enough to load quickly online. You can save the file as an HD video that will play on the web and on mobile devices such as the iPhone and iPad.

Saving Videos with Premiere Elements

If you edit your videos in Adobe Premiere Elements (available for Mac and Windows), you'll need to stay on your toes during the export process to avoid the software's suboptimal default options. Premier Elements does let you upload videos to YouTube and Facebook with one click—which is tempting (*Figure* 10.1). However, the default setting for the one-click upload option encodes files in the dreaded Adobe Flash format, which Apple does not support for its mobile devices. Do it this way, and your video will be seen on the web version of YouTube in low quality.

In general, I try to steer clear of one-click upload options. They sound good in theory, but end up taking more time in the long run. For example, after a file has been compressed, sometimes there's a hiccup in the uploading process and you have to start all over again. Another potential problem with using the one-click option: you won't have the finished file on your hard drive. What if you want to post it somewhere else, later on down the road? So, I believe in avoiding the one-click upload and saving files to a specific place on your hard drive.

Premiere Elements offers a host of export options, from Flash to MPEG (for DVDs) to QuickTime. Select the Computer option in the Share tab to review the options. Be sure to choose QuickTime, and look to advanced settings to make sure you get a good, full-size high-definition file that will look great on the web.

(Premiere Elements 10 defaults to standard definition!) Select the Video tab in the Export Settings dialog box to change the quality settings. Under Video Codec choices, choose the H.264 option and change the Width in the Basic Settings to 1,920 if you're shooting in 1080p HD (Figure 10.2).

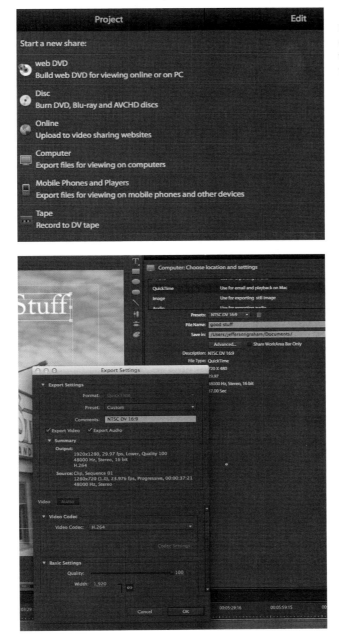

Figure 10.1 Just be wary of one-click options for exporting such as those shown here. Instead, save the file to your hard drive.

Figure 10.2 Export options in Premiere Elements.

Figure 10.3 Export your video in iMovie with H.264 settings.

Saving Files in iMovie

To export a video in iMovie, here's all you need to do:

- Choose Export Movie using QuickTime, from the Share menu.
- Click the Options tab and make sure the Settings are H.264 for Compression Type and at least 1280x720 for Size, which is great for online playback.
- Click Save As and name the file (*Figure 10.3*).
- Choose the destination (desktop, external hard drive, etc.).

Exporting in Final Cut Pro X

When upgrading Final Cut Pro 7 to version X, Apple greatly simplified the export process. Version 7 offered so many choices it was mind-numbing. In the end, I always just scrolled through to find H.264. In FCP X, I just click Share from the menu, and choose Apple Devices. Then I opt for the iPad choice, which gives me a good size 1280x720 file that will load quickly on the web, and play well on recent iPhones, iPods, and iPads as well (*Figure 10.4*).

Finding a File in the Future

It's key to think about where you save your video files. When you visit a site such as YouTube or Facebook to upload files, you can't get anywhere if you don't know where your videos are on your hard drive.

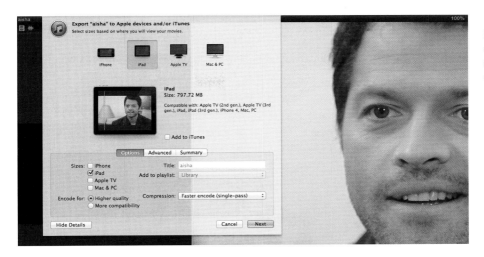

Figure 10.4 You can export quickly to a variety of Apple devices.

Figure 10.5 Not only is Vimeo a great video playback website, but it offers great resources on compression.

Many people like to save their files on the Desktop, just because they know they'll be able to find them. In Adobe Premiere Elements, the default location for saving files is the Documents folder; iMovie sometimes steers you to the Movie folder. I direct my exported videos to the folder I created for the project. That way, I know exactly where they are.

Best Source for Answers to Compression Questions

Filmmakers favor the Vimeo website (*Figure 10.5*), which features an arty presentation, tons of camera-geek tech videos, and the invaluable Video 101 series of short videos on lighting, photography, videography, and video editing. It's also the absolute best place online to answer any questions that arise about compression when exporting your videos (vimeo.com/help/compression).

The site has guides on how to export your video using every conceivable video-editing program, from iMovie and Movie Maker to Premiere Elements, Final Cut Pro, and programs you might have never heard of, such as Handbrake, VisualHub, and Camtasia.

YouTube Rules

YouTube offers a few compression tips of its own, but they are nowhere near as useful as those on Vimeo's page. The interesting thing about YouTube, however, is that it gained popularity in its infancy because the videos could always be viewed quickly—with little buffering or hiccupping issues as you would get elsewhere on the web. That's because YouTube initially transcoded all uploaded videos into the lower-quality Flash format. The good news: quick load times. The bad news: not-so-hot video quality.

YouTube has come a long way since then. Encouraged by, I believe, the fine HD presentation at Vimeo, YouTube now defaults to HD in the full 16:9 aspect ratio you get on flat-panel TVs—even if a video isn't uploaded in high definition. (Standard Definition videos in the 4:3 aspect ratio display with a little box around them so everything can fit.)

As a viewer, you can either watch the video in a small box or, if you have a great Internet connection, choose the Large or Full Screen player options and take advantage of the full HD (*Figure 10.6*). You can also choose whether to watch in 480p (small), 720p (medium,) or full 1080p HD (large) size. Most of the HD videos are in the slightly lower 720p category, although, some of the YouTubers you've met here in *Video Nation*—such as Valentino Trevino from "Val's Art Diary" and Joe Penna, the Mystery Guitar Man—do offer select videos in 1080p. My "Talking Tech" videos for *USA TODAY* are in 720p.

Figure 10.6 Playback on YouTube is very good today and you can view videos in full 1080p HD.

Final Check

Once the video is exported, confirm that you're really, truly finished. Take a good look all the way through the exported video. Are there any mistakes? The answer is, probably, yes. Perhaps a transition should run a second or two longer. Or maybe a name is misspelled. I confess that I do two or three exports every time before I get it right.

After making the corrections and re-exporting the video, you should be happy and satisfied. Great. Now comes a word of warning. If you ever want to go back and work on the video again, make sure all those files are in the exact same place, because otherwise, you're doomed.

For example, when editing the project—let's call it "Video Nation"—you are working from a folder of video files that are on an external hard drive. (If you followed my suggestion, that is. Otherwise, they may be on your hard drive.) Let's say you added some screen shots you downloaded from the Internet that ended up on your Desktop. And then you found a song on iTunes that went into the Downloads folder. (This is a bad workflow, by the way. Everything related to a project should be stored in the same folder. But I'm assuming you're sometimes as sloppy as I am.) Now, three weeks have gone by, and you deleted the screen shots from the Desktop and moved the song to your Music folder. Then you open the project again to tweak it. Guess what—red marks all over it report that files are missing.

To ensure that you can work on a video again later, be sure to store all the files in the same easy-to-locate folder to begin with. And if you don't, make sure you don't delete anything from the project until you can confirm that you never, ever want to work on it again.

UPLOADING VIDEOS TO THE WEB

Now for the simplest part of the process—uploading videos. Let's start by looking at the various places you can upload videos. Then I'll walk you through the process up uploading your videos to YouTube.

A Home for Your Masterpieces

The two most popular places to view online video are YouTube and Facebook. The good news about YouTube is that you can join its AdSense program and receive a cut of the ad revenues. (See the "Make Some Money: Try AdSense" sidebar later in this section.) So the more views you get, the more potential you have to make money.

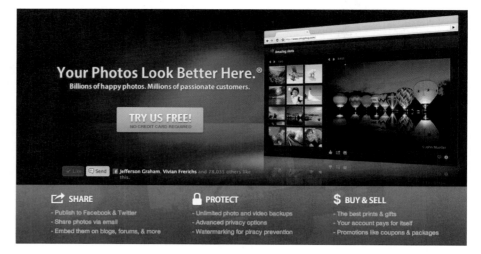

Figure 10.7
Smugmug is a good option for professional-looking videos without ads.

You could post the video on Facebook as well, but you're better off sharing the YouTube video with Facebook directly, so that each view counts as a YouTube click. Vimeo is a great site as well, and your stuff will look great. If you run a business, you can pay an annual subscription fee, which removes the Vimeo branding and offers a more professional look. Another option is the photo- and video-sharing site Smugmug (*Figure 10.7*), where you can pay either $60 or $150 per year to have your video seen without ads.

TIP Posting to Vimeo and Smugmug also archives your work. If your hard drive crashes, you can just go to Vimeo or Smugmug and download the files in full resolution. I'm a member of both services. In effect, Vimeo is my backup hard drive for all my video work.

Another advantage of posting on Vimeo and YouTube is that you can watch those videos on TV. Many new "smart" TVs have accessory "channels" that can access specific Internet sites, such as Vimeo, as do set-top boxes such as the Roku and networked Blu-ray players.

- Vimeo is on Apple TV and the Roku, Samsung, Vizio, and Panasonic smart TVs.
- YouTube is on Apple TV and Google TV; smart TVs from LG, Panasonic, Sony, and Samsung; and the Sony PlayStation gaming device.

More devices support these sites all the time.

MAKE SOME MONEY: TRY ADSENSE

Anyone can apply to and be accepted by AdSense, Google's program that places ads all over the Internet—including on blogs and YouTube (*Figure 10.8*). To get started, go to google.com/adsense, fill out the form, and give them your banking information.

Now, when you post videos on YouTube, AdSense ads will start popping up, and you'll get a cut of the action. Google will start putting money directly into your account—even for the least-viewed videos. Making money with AdSense is a numbers game: The more videos you post, the better shot you have at bringing in the bucks.

If you're interested in getting a better revenue split from Google—and don't mind your creation being littered with ads—YouTube's Partner program should be your end goal. For Partners, YouTube pays out at least 51 percent of the ad revenues to the creators.

To get in the Partner program, you need to reach a certain number of views for your videos. YouTube won't spell out the criteria for accepting you as a Partner, but it generally comes down to this: You need to make videos often and people need to watch them—in big numbers. Various writers online have speculated that you need a cumulative total of hundreds of thousands of views to get in. Apply at youtube.com/partner.

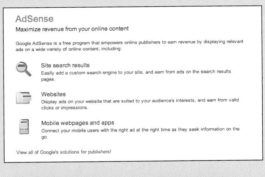

Figure 10.8 AdSense adds commissions based on video views to your bank account.

Uploading to YouTube and Creating Your Channel

To get started with YouTube, you'll be asked to create and name your channel. If you've already done this, login with your Google ID. (Old YouTube IDs no longer work—Google has migrated users to its credential system.) Think of something memorable that you'll want to live with for many years. Then, simply look for the Upload tab and click it. Select the video you want and start the process. The speed with which it reaches YouTube depends on the size of the video and the speed of your Internet connection. It usually takes me 5 to 15 minutes to upload a 250 MB file, but I have a really good connection via Verizon's FIOS service.

Learn how to create a YouTube channel by watching the video at www.peachpit.com/videonation.

Creating a Title

While a video is uploading, you can get busy creating its title. Give the video a title that helps users find it easily in Google and YouTube searches. Add tags to help with the search the process. (A title such as "My First YouTube Video" would obviously get you nowhere in terms of searches and views.)

Val from "Val's Art Diary," whom we met in Chapter 6, says the title creation is the most important thing you will do to get the word out about your video (*Figure 10.9*).

"YouTube will reward you if you spend time to tag your video properly," she says. "YouTube will reward you tenfold if you do that and your video happens to be relevant to what the Internet is talking about. This is where many people discover that the topical nature of their videos plays a larger role than all the fancy production tools and techniques."

Maybe you're not making topical videos that play off the news, and you're just looking to make and share a small business video. You still want to be seen, right? So, in the case of the local bookshop in Chapter 6, I'd title it with the name and subject "Manhattan Beach {pages} Bookstore Lisa See Book Signing." This way, you get the name of the business and location front and center, and you mention an author who signed books at the shop. These three items are vital if you want Google to find your business during a local search. Obviously, by including "Manhattan Beach" and "books" in the subject line, your video is likelier to be discovered in a Google search for a local bookstore. And, if someone is interested in Lisa See, and they happen to live in the South Bay area of Los Angeles, they now know that authors like See visit a bookstore they may not have known existed.

Figure 10.9 Creative yet accurate titles will make your videos stand out.

Shooting Video with Canon 5D Mark II and 7D | Redrock Micro Accessories | Talking Tech

EOS
5D

USA TODAY

Subscribe · 153 videos ▾

0:03 / 3:13

Like · Add to ▾ · Share

544,695

More from talkingtech's uploads

Figure 10.10
Try picking a title
that matches what
is hot or current in
viewers' searches.

I hit upon Val's trick about timing your videos to current events in early 2010, when I did a *USA TODAY* piece on Redrock Micro, a small company that makes rigs that help steady DSLR cameras. I posted the video on our "Talking Tech" channel on YouTube, titled it "Shooting Video with the Canon 5D Mark II and 7D," and it quickly became one of our most popular YouTube videos ever, reaping more than 500,000 views (*Figure 10.10*). I didn't get the viewers because I made a great video; I got them simply because I had a good, timely title. Shooting video on DSLRs was relatively new then, and folks were searching for any sort of tips they could find on how to do it. This video was available early and Google discovered it, so when folks searched for "shooting video with the Canon 5D Mark II" or words to that effect, my video tended to pop right up.

So there's something to be said for a good, timely title.

Categories

When posting a video, YouTube asks you to select a category for it to be listed in. The categories are a subjective list that includes options such as Auto, Comedy, Education, and Entertainment. Interestingly, it does not include Business. So if that's your category, just choose whatever seems most appropriate. If you have a business video that's entertaining, stick it in Entertainment.

YouTube asks you to categorize your video so it knows where to put it. On the YouTube home page, channels are divided into these various categories to help users with browsing. When you visit, you'll see a collection of comedy, education, science/tech videos, and more (*Figure 10.11*). And hopefully your video is in there.

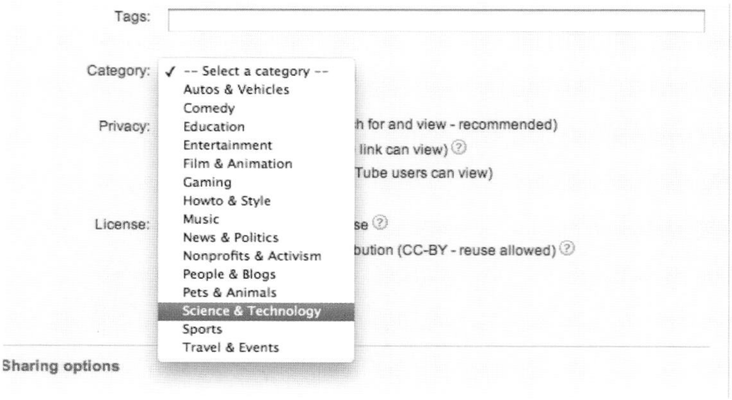

Figure 10.11 Categories help keep YouTube videos organized and easy to find.

Tags:

Category: ✓ -- Select a category --
Autos & Vehicles
Comedy
Education
Entertainment
Film & Animation
Gaming
Howto & Style
Music
News & Politics
Nonprofits & Activism
People & Blogs
Pets & Animals
Science & Technology
Sports
Travel & Events

Privacy:

License:

Sharing options

Importance of Words

If you have a website and want it to do really well on Google searches, there are three things you need to do.

1 Give it a good, relevant title, using descriptive text that tells Google exactly what you're selling.

2 Use relevant keywords—the words folks would use in a search to find a site like yours.

3 Add a well-written description that tells people what you've got.

Because YouTube is owned by Google, you can expect the same of its video site. Start with a great title, give it a category, and then write a good description of the video. Keep in mind that the words you use are what will display in Google (if the search engine decides to add your site to the index).

Remember the hypothetical blogger from Greateats we met in Chapter 5—the one who went to meet the owner of the Good Stuff Restaurant? For her video, I would use the words "Greateats: Redondo Beach Restaurant Review" in the title. The description would then say, "Los Angeles food blogger Goodeats visits Redondo Beach's Good Stuff Restaurant and meets owner Cris Bennett. Mr. Good Stuff discusses his most popular dishes, which include the breakfast salad, fish tacos, and penne pasta."

This description is to the point and includes several clues for Google. The name of the blog is front and center, as is the restaurant name of Good Stuff and the location of Redondo Beach. Those are three searchable items, as are the names of the dishes. For good measure, I'd put a link on the Greateats name, which is as simple as typing it as http://greateats.com.

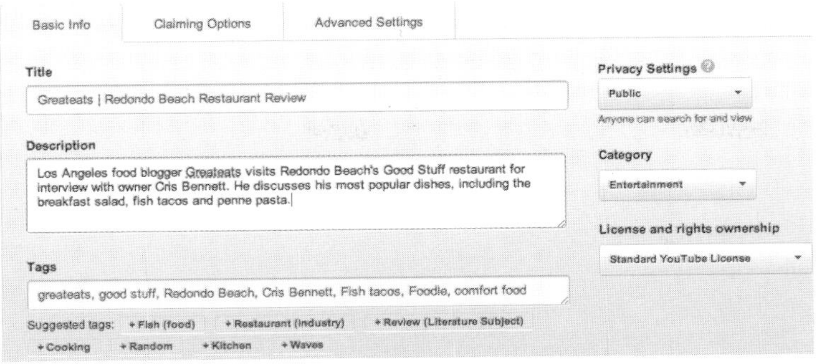

Figure 10.12 Adding tags to videos is *not*, in fact, a waste a time.

Just adding the *http://* instructs YouTube to put a link on it. The link will help the blog show up, possibly, in Google searches, and also could help you with the Google index. (More on that in a minute.)

Tagging

It's now time to finish up with the last piece of business—creating tags, also known as keywords. Throwing all those tags at the bottom of a video seems like a real waste of time, right (*Figure 10.12*)? What's the point? Again, it's so Google and YouTube can search your videos and show them to the world. It's another way to help them categorize the video, both for viewers and advertisers. For the Greateats Good Stuff video, my tags would be: Greateats, Good Stuff, Redondo Beach, Cris Bennett, restaurant, fish tacos, foodie, comfort food, and breakfast salad.

More on Links

When Larry Page and Sergey Brin started Google in 1996, their better take on a search engine was a revelation. Search results became more accurate and swifter than those from previous search engines such as Yahoo, MSN, and Alta Vista. Basically, their formula consisted of a popularity contest. If your site is linked to by others—in other words, if your site got referenced by high-quality sites such as *The New York Times*, slashdot, and AOL—you could rest assured that you were going to zip to the top of the Google rankings. And thus, as Google gained popularity, people fought hard to have others linking to their sites. Sometimes it happens naturally—so many people like your site that they link to it in a blog post, perhaps. Other times, it's not so natural—many shady firms sell links from others in hopes of gaming the Google search engine. Sometimes it works, but if Google catches it, you'll be thrown off the site. So you want to steer clear of that.

Figure 10.13 Put a link to your site somewhere prominent in the video description.

When writing your video's description, I suggest you start the first link with a link to your site (*Figure 10.13*). Then, hope that others join in. We'll explore other ways to get links in the next section.

SCREAM IT TO THE WORLD

Your video is uploaded with great eye-catching words in the title, a description, and keywords that will all help people find it.

So now you just sit back and wait for the acclaim, right? Not so fast.

You need to consider the basic troika of any good marketer's advertising— YouTube, Facebook, and Twitter. For effective promotion, you need to use all three plus some additional shoe leather of your own—blogging, working your email list, leaving notes on forums, and the like.

Subscriptions

To help build an audience, many YouTubers push hard for folks to subscribe to their channel (*Figure 10.14*). That way, every time you post a new video, an alert about the video's arrival goes out to all of your subscribers. This gives you a ready audience willing to click on your latest masterpiece.

My mom, whom you met in Chapter 8, has 12,000 subscribers, which isn't a bad number. But the most subscribed-to channel is from Ray William Johnson, who has more than 5 million subscribers for his saucy comedy videos. All he has to do is post a new video, and some 5 million folks get an alert. What are the chances that a decent number of them tune in? Well, even if it's only 1 percent, that's still a nice instant viewership of 50,000.

Figure 10.14 A good way to get people to subscribe to your channel is with a prominent Subscribe button.

Figure 10.15 At more than 1.6 billion, the number of views Ray William Johnson receives is staggering.

Views

The name of the game at YouTube is views. How many people are watching your videos?

It's just like TV and the Nielsen ratings. Why is "Dancing with the Stars" a smash hit? It has a massive audience. You want to get into the Partner program? You need lots of views for your videos. You want to brag to your friends about how you're doing on YouTube? There's only one metric that counts: views.

Ray William Johnson not only has the most subscribed-to channel, but he is also the most seen YouTube partner (as of 2012). His aggregate view count tops 1.7 billion (*Figure 10.15*)!

Making It Viral

Ariana Grande, a young 18-year-old actress from the Nickelodeon TV show "Victorious," was bored one afternoon at home, so she went into her bedroom, turned on her webcam, and started singing Adele's "Rolling in the Deep," a cappella, directly into the computer.

She thought it was cute, so she posted it on YouTube.

Grande has an active fan base of 1.7 million fans who check her out on Twitter, and she's big on other social networks such as Instagram, too. But the response to her YouTube video—28 million views—shocked her.

"It's just one of those things," she says. "It just went viral and took off, with a life of its own." She said, "Had I known it would get so many views, I would have worked harder and learned all the words to the song."

That's the thing about viral videos. No one knows exactly what the magic formula is. Piano-playing cats? Dogs doing stunts? Babies doing the darndest things (*Figure 10.16*)? Find something that works and people will enjoy passing it along in emails and recommending it on blogs.

I would love to give you a list of five things you could do to ensure that your video goes viral. But if I knew the magic formula, I wouldn't be writing books—I'd be producing viral videos and making a fortune!

Business consultant Jeff Korhan, on his small business blog, cites this overly simplistic formula: "The easiest way to have your video go viral is to video someone doing something incredibly stupid."

Figure 10.16
The "Charlie Bit My Finger" video was viewed more than 439 million times.

This advice from an article in *Business Insider* by James DuJulio is more useful: "Create lots of videos (the more you make, the better the chances people will find you), make them funny (that always works in viral), and opt for the parody approach, especially if you can make fun of something that's topical. If you can act quickly to people at the right time, you've got a chance at some resonance."

Easier said than done, but there's a reason why YouTube is littered with highly viewed parody videos, usually of music videos and news events.

Tweaking Your Channel

Once you've posted several videos on your YouTube channel, you'll want to tweak the layout and customize it to make it look more impressive.

Click the Edit Channel tab to start the process. If you know Photoshop, or have a friend who does, make a banner for your channel to display across the top of the screen. (Online free alternatives are plenty—try Pixlr or Gimp.) I made the "Talking Tech" banner at 900 pixels wide and 150 tall, and then uploaded it. I chose a banner height of 75. You can also choose the background color for your channel, fine-tune the channel description and tags, and pick the layout you like best (*Figure 10.17*).

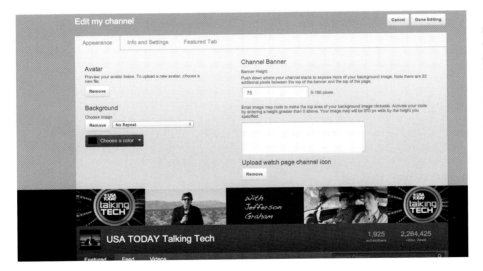

Figure 10.17
Create an avatar (your photo or likeness), a background, and a channel banner to spiff up your YouTube channel.

Figure 10.18
Embed your link
so your videos are
easy to share.

Embeds

Using "embeds" for sharing YouTube links across the web are a great way to show YouTube love (*Figure 10.18*). You can cut and paste Embed codes into blogs. Putting your YouTube videos on Facebook is even easier. Just copy and paste the URL into Facebook's Status Update box on your profile page.

Embeds are another factor Google uses in determining the popularity of your video.

Likes

As with Facebook, YouTube viewers are asked to click a Like button under videos and leave star ratings (*Figure 10.19*). This is another popularity factor Google considers.

Comments

A video with lots of discussion shows Google there's something going on that is worthy of taking notice. But you better have a thick skin. In my experience, YouTube viewers can be really nasty, much more so than on other sites (even if they are nice to my mother).

Figure 10.19 Google looks at how many Likes
you receive for your channel in determining
your popularity.

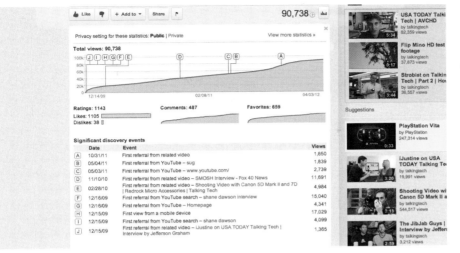

Figure 10.20
Learning more about how your videos are referred helps you understand your audience and their behaviors.

Fun Stuff

Under each YouTube video the [name] tab shows how your video has been found and where it is embedded. For example, my "Shooting Video on the Canon 5D Mark II" video, the one with more than 500,000 YouTube views, shows that it was mostly discovered in Google searches. A more recent video—my "Talking Tech" video interview with "Mad Men's" Christina Hendricks, shows referrals from Hendricks' fan sites, online searches for the actress, and overflows from folks watching the Canon 5D video (*Figure 10.20*).

Facebook

Every video you make that goes on YouTube can also be placed on Facebook, where you can discuss it with your family, friends, and subscribers in what is generally a more supportive setting. Reason: Nobody there is hiding under an anonymous name.

On Facebook, you're playing the word-of-mouth game with the largest social network in the world—almost 1 billion folks. You're starting with your friends, who you hope will like the video and pass it onto their wider circle of friends. As we saw in the "Taking It to the Web" section in Chapter 2, videos become viral when they move outside your initial Facebook page and get reposted.

TIP For a great resource on this topic, look at *Grouped: How Small Groups of Friends are the Key to Influence on the Social Web* by Paul Adams, global brand experience manager at Facebook (New Riders, 2012).

Figure 10.21 Check out TwitVid at www.twitvid.com for posting videos on Twitter as well.

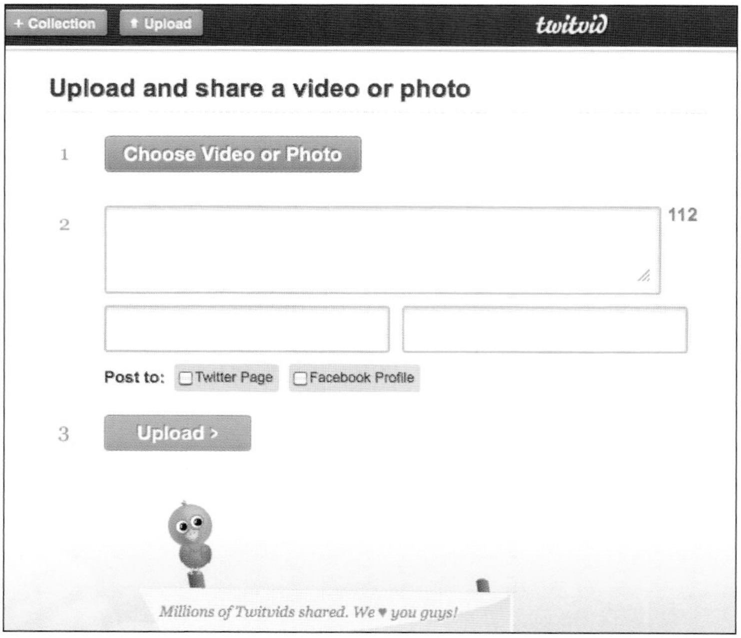

Twitter

If you haven't already, sign up for Twitter and become an active member of the community. Use the TwitVid service to start posting your online videos, which gets your videos on Twitter (*Figure 10.21*).

Each Tweet of information sent can be up to 140 characters long. You can send photos, videos and conversations directly in Tweets. The Twitter website describes how it can be used by business owners in this way:

"Twitter connects businesses to customers in real time—and businesses use Twitter to quickly share information with people interested in their products and services, gather real-time market intelligence and feedback, and build relationships with customers, partners and influencers. From brand lift to CRM to direct sales, Twitter offers businesses an easy way to reach an engaged audience."

You can read more about Twitter and learn how to use it by visiting www.twitter.com/about.

Summing It Up

So there you have it. You made a video, uploaded it, and now, we hope, it's being seen by thousands of people. You learned that editing video not only isn't bad, it's a whole lot of fun!

I hope the skills I've shared help make your videos at least a little better—if not markedly improved. And, if you're a businessperson, I'd love to hear that you've raised your community profile and started to grow your business with video.

But let's not stop there.

I hope you get so excited about the possibilities of making videos that you'll at least add a second camera, if not a third, to your shoots.

Please keep in touch with me, let me know how it's going, and hit me with any questions. I'll try to answer as many of them as I can. Just promise me you'll be nice to me on YouTube!

You can also find me here:

- Tech.usatoday.com
- Twitter: @jeffersongraham
- Facebook.com/jeffersongraham

It's been a blast sharing my knowledge with you and diving into my all-time favorite subject. I hope you all enjoyed it as much as I did.

So until next time, I'm Jefferson Graham, reporting from Los Angeles for *Video Nation*.

32

Jefferson's concluding remarks can also be found in the video at www.peachpit.com/videonation.

INDEX

Audio-Technica ATR3350 lavalier mic, 64
AVCHD clips, warning about, 50

B

B&H website, 49
"Baby" parody, 36–38
backgrounds, replacing, 199–201
backing up files, 154
Baig, Ed, 4
banking business, making videos for, 31
Bennett, Cris, 96, 98–99, 132, 214
Bertinelli, Valerie, 8, 113
Bescor TH-770 High-Performance tripod, 69
Bieber, Justin, 35
Black Universal Bracket Adapter Mount, 72
Bloggie Live HD camcorder, 50–51
boardroom shots, avoiding, 110
Boedigheimer, Dane, *See also* Annoying Orange
    44–45, 146
brainstorming. *See* ideas
Brin, Sergey, 215
B-roll
    adding to editing workflow, 159–160
    collecting on location, 129–130
    defined, 11
    preplanning, 100–101
    taking for one-camera shoots, 141
    using, 11
    using in Facebook interview, 16–17
Brooks, Mel, 24
business videos
    advertorials, 20
    banking, 31
    content to avoid, 29

dry cleaning, 31
effective approaches, 28
food, 31
home buyer videos, 30
garden store example, 27
ideas for, 31
photography software, 32–33
promoting, 27
sell subtly, 29
shooting, 131-132
smaill-business video, 27
speaking to customers, 28
taking video to the web, 28

C

camcorders. *See also* video cameras
    point-and-shoot, 50–51
    using, 90–91
camera bag, 77
camera mounts
    monopods, 69
    steadicams, 71
    tiny tripods, 68
    tripods, 68–69
camera positions, planning, 97
cameras. *See also* one-camera shoots;
        three-camera shoots; two-camera shoots;
        video cameras
    Canon, 56-57
    digital SLRs, 55–57
    DSLR, 88–89
    GoPro, 58
    iPad, 54–55
    iPhone, 54